Under The Hen's Bottom

Memoirs from an Ulster childhood

Wendy Breckon

Dedication

To my supportive, kind husband Pete who never minds
leaving his shed for a story.

To my amazing sons Sam and Oliver, daughter in law Lorraine,
and fabulous grandsons Finn and Noah.

To dear Mum, Michael and Emily.

To brother-in-law Alan, Sarah, Julia; Mark, Linda and family.

To my lovely cousins in Northern Ireland and dear Aunty Irene
and Aunty Mabel. Thanks for my childhood memories.

To my close friends of many years, Chris and John, Rosemary
and Dave, Gloria and Mac, Pat and Roger, Jed and Avril, Lorna
and David, Sue MacFayden and Pet and Roger Taylor.

To Denise and Mike Rodway.

To my writing friend Richard Green and a special mention
to Frances Colville, friend, mentor and excellent proof reader.
I appreciate your great efforts.

Finally to Tracey and Simon West for giving me
the opportunity to put my words into print.

Thank you!

Foreword
Going Forward

Writing has always been part of my life. An exquisite joy. My raison d'être. In some of the stories you will read about a young girl who scribbled furiously on a page. From an early age, a pencil and pen became very important. Collecting thoughts and ideas in order to write poetry or stories. I was a prolific creator of rhymes. At primary school I composed many poems and was full of delight when the teacher read them out in class.

At the age of eight in County Down, an adult patted me on the head once and asked what I wanted to be when I grew up. With a determined toss of the blond plaits, I replied with the firm answer, 'a writer'. They were taken aback! Not quite the expected response. So, here I am at sixty something achieving my dream. Never too late! Success feels like sniffing the sweetest flower on the stem, or taking the first nibble out of a delicious cake. Simply fabulous! And let's not forget the iconic image of biting a cherry. Except in my case, I shall be greedy and ask for two.

When my family crossed over the sea to England in 1968 a couple of our personal tea chests disappeared. One of life's mysteries. I never saw those special folders with my prized poetry in ever again. This didn't deter me. A slight setback. I've had much worse. I just kept on scribbling furiously, as I coped with my new and strange environment.

Over the years I have composed many articles, stories and rhymes, written for a local newspaper, a London 'freebie' and a successful on-line magazine. But, 'Under The Hen's Bottom', originated from having to cope with the effects of long term illness. This collection of quirky, amusing tales means everything to me. I focused… tried not to think about the things I could not do and relived my quirky childhood experiences.

For those of you coping with something similar or maybe some other life changing experience, pick up a pen. Any pen or a pencil. Get creative! Rip out a page or even treat yourself to a jazzy notebook. I favour a touch of humour, a blitz of sparkle or an inspirational message on the front cover. Start scribbling! Don't wait! There's nothing like today. Record your thoughts, ideas, a bit of a story or even a rant. Why? Because this helps. It's therapeutic. Sniff the sea, linger through the park or saunter through the countryside. Find a place of calm. Expressing yourself makes life a little better. Issues easier to deal with. Watch the words; your words tumbling in front of you. Be pleasantly surprised. You're in charge! Create patterns on the blank page. Write occasionally when the mood takes you or scribble furiously until your fingers explode. It's your choice. Accept some days you might not be able to and that's fine.

Being able to communicate my thoughts has helped me so much in life; with the everyday and the occasional. There will be good and bad days. Enjoy the kind people who wander into your life. Keep going... I did... be inspired by what you can do. I attended a memoir workshop with a brilliant tutor, a few years ago, met other writers and never looked back. Everyone has a tale to tell, an amusing anecdote or experience. You don't have to share these with others unless you want to. That's important. Read it privately to someone you trust, a friend, a parent or maybe a close colleague. I'm a keen advocate of the story read out loud. Sometimes... why not read the words out loud to yourself, when the house is empty and still. This is equally empowering. You don't always need an audience.

Words are a healer, a delight and always cathartic. You'll be surprised at their power! Why not start writing your own piece of magic now. As always what you keep inside or talk about is totally up to you.

Good Luck, Wendy x

1

Nearly Born in a Hedge

"Push!"

"I can't."

"Push a little bit harder. It almost started."

"I'll try."

The antiquated engine spluttered and backfired twice, scattering curious creatures in its path. The young, dark-haired woman gave the biggest push ever and the black Austin Riley decided to start. The jerky sound of the motor was sweet music to my dad's ears. He smiled, lit up a cigarette and patted the bonnet in appreciation. My mother clutched her stomach and tried not to give birth there and then, in the middle of a thorny hedgerow in County Down.

"Yes! Well done! Knew you could do it."

"I don't think I should be pushing anything... *I'm having a baby!*"

"Jump in. I'll get you there in no time. No need to make a fuss."

The explosive roaring of the engine would have been heard for miles around. The buzz was enough to unsettle the group of cows idly gazing over the hedge and a flock of geese ambling down Drumiller Lane. The gentle rolling Ulster hills with their fields of clover and buttercups surrounded the cottages dotted here and there. The warm September sun glinted on the curved metal, as the two people inside bounced round corners, past Granny and Grandad's home, Hillside Cottage, on the right, and shook all the way to the local hospital. My mother clung onto the door handle, feeling grateful that her first baby was not going to be born in a hedge after all. On seeing her face in the mirror, my dad shouted, "Not long now love. Hold on. Nearly there." As usual, he was brimming with confidence.

Home for my mother and father at that time in 1952 was a ramshackle cottage right up in the hills. Rampant ivy and brambles scrambling up the walls. An inglenook fireplace with a shivery outside privy. Totally unsuitable for a person about to give birth! Eventually, as this was only a temporary measure, they moved down to a house in the village while I was still a baby. Lots of space for a young family and the chance to grow vegetables and flowers.

One morning, eight months earlier on a crisp January day, the tiny village shop had been buzzing with gossip. There were the usual whispers about people who had left the village, farmers whose wayward cows had stopped producing milk and the hefty price someone had paid for a tractor. Local women, young and old, were collecting their Woman's Weeklies and knitting wool patterns. Baskets of local provisions, with fresh Irish cheese and ham, nestled in greaseproof paper, tied with string, alongside jars of Bovril and tins of condensed milk. These swung on their arms as they caught up with all the latest news. My mother recalls feeling faint and woozy amongst the sawdust, the sweet smell of caramel toffees and thick slices of newly cut bacon. She didn't realise at the time that she might be expecting a child. As she sat on a chair clinging to her handbag, the older women winked and nodded at her and to each other. A quiet moment for them to reminisce about happy days gone-by.

The Austin Riley hurtled down the lanes with magical powers, past the dirty tractors and haycarts. Eventually to my mother's relief, the car pulled sharply into Banbridge hospital, and she, surprisingly, was still in one piece. And so… a little girl was born in a small town in County Down. Wendy Elizabeth. 8lbs 8oz. 29th September 1952. Wendy, after one of the characters in 'Peter Pan', a popular name in the 1950s and Elizabeth, after my great grandmother.

"We can't believe your poor wife had to do all that pushing and shoving when she was about to give birth. You should feel ashamed of yourself. First baby too! Make sure you've got a car that starts next time," said the doctor.

Dad was suitably chastened and peeped out from his hiding place behind the screen. He hadn't been expecting a scolding so didn't know what to say. The midwife and nurses gave him stern glances and wiggled their fingers, but at least he wasn't chased down the corridor with a clipboard and stethoscope. He hung around sheepishly, doing exactly what they told him.

My grandad's mother from Manchester paid a visit fairly soon to meet the bonny arrival. She was delighted to cuddle the tiny bundle in her arms. The slim birdlike figure leant against the black Austin Riley and said to all, "I never thought I'd live to see this day."

I spent my early years, like many others, tucked up in a sturdy cream carriage pram, peeping over the covers at those looking in. Strange and familiar faces nodded with approval making those peculiar expressions only reserved for babies. Tiny children tried to poke with inquisitive fingers whilst their parents weren't looking. It was so warm and cosy, with Whisky our black cat always looking for an opportunity to sneak inside. Watching the world passing by... being pushed here and there... waiting patiently for what might lie ahead... in a special place called Ulster. My mother regularly manoeuvred her new daughter up Drumiller Lane to see her husband's parents. It was only a short walk past the hedgerows, where tiny birds collected twigs for their nest and honey bees buzzed behind in the clover. Opposite the farmhouse uncles and loyal friends helped with the harvest, while an ancient tractor ploughed the fields, followed by the usual flock of squawking birds. Thermos flasks were swigged at intervals and doorstep sandwiches shoved into wide hungry mouths. As a sleeping baby I was often parked up near the haystacks oblivious to the family activity. When I was old enough, I foraged and explored these natural surroundings, with the help of Granny's favourite book, 'Eyes And No Eyes', given to her as a Sunday School prize in 1902 for excellent attendance. The beautiful sketches of flowers, plants and creatures of the countryside were magic to my creative mind.

One of my favourite pastimes was making a beeline for our very docile 'moggy'. He used to lie perfectly still as I dressed him up in all my dolls' clothes. Looking resplendent in smocked dresses, lacy bonnets and other dazzling items, Whisky settled himself under the covers, while I pushed him in my own tiny pram. Off I toddled with my captive creature, round the perimeter of the sizeable field with the shabby wooden hut in the corner which sold sweets. Neighbours and passersby would smile and wave occasionally at the twitching ears and dark whiskers. Eventually he would decide enough was enough! Within seconds Whisky's mad scramble for fresh air resulted in a gigantic leap from my second-hand pram.

"Well... Wendy. The cat lasted five seconds longer than last time," my mother laughed, watching as Whisky darted up the lane and zigzagged through the cornfield. I wasn't very old but I do remember the poor creature wearing two white bootees, a blue lacy bonnet and trailing a floral dress behind him.

"I think it's time to give him a rest," came the suggestion one day and I reluctantly agreed to take her advice. When my baby brother was old enough to be pushed, Whisky was free! He didn't have to worry about a small girl pursuing him, as I could now push the real thing up and down the field. What relief for his feline credibility! My mum loved to stand by the open window in the upstairs bedroom. She would call his name and usually as he was hungry, he would stop sniffing for rabbits and return home. She recalls our cat weaving like a pack of tumbling dominoes through the golden corn, not content until his paws were knee-deep in a bowl of cat food. Sadly it wasn't long before he disappeared for ever. My parents never knew what happened to him but everyone missed his quirky company. We took a while to get over our loss. From an early age I adored animals of all kinds. Maybe one exception being made for fluttering hens... elaborated on in a future story. Farmyard creatures were to be chased or be chased by, stroked, lifted up and carried... or sat on!

My parents owned two dogs, mother and daughter. OB the former, had been plucked and rescued from a basket of sickly puppies in a backstreet window. He like the others was suffering from severe malnutrition, but they could only take one. Mum and Dad nursed him back to good health, with great devotion. The secret was heaped spoonfuls of the now vintage Benger's food powder. She was a docile, gentle black and white collie, who unfortunately one day gave birth to a very bossy puppy. Brandy was a golden haired half sheepdog who gobbled all the food up before her mother could even sniff it. She could be a little aggressive and always had to be in charge. Poor OB had wandered into the wrong farmyard one morning and got pregnant. One day I put forward a proposition to my mother. I smile now when I recall the words, because I have no idea where the thoughts originated from.

"I wish the dogs were mine. I want to own them completely."

"Well... okay that's fine," came the bemused reply. "So you have to do everything. Feed them, brush their coats, take them for a walk."

For a few days I became a dutiful pet owner, and relished the newfound responsibility. On the fourth day my unhappy face said it all.

"Mummy!"

"Yes Wendy?"

"Can you take them back now? I don't want to own them anymore."

The laughter from the front sitting room lasted for ages. I was delighted that my life could now return to normal.

As a five year old the journey to school seemed never-ending. As I skipped on the pavements through our little village, our faithful cat, until his disappearance, would follow us and wait in a hedge for my mother's return. Pretty pebble-dashed cottages looked delightful on the left and on the right the River Bann glided past. This is where my grandad loved to sit and fish. With lingering dragonflies and ducks peering out of the reeds, he would cast his line and stare for hours into the blue green water. The usual woodbine dangling on the edge of his lip as he wobbled on a dark green fishing stool. Sometimes, I would drift around him waiting for a lucky catch and a soupcon of rare conversation. The Ulster sun high in the sky and the prickly heat exploding on our backs.

In the 1950s all children held their mother's hand, (it was rarely fathers) as we made our way slowly up to Scarva County Primary school, dragging our Clarks' sandals when the hill approached. One morning in the holidays when my toddler brother was being pushed in the same carriage pram, my mum stopped to use the red phone box at the top of the street. This was the original push button A and B system where one's pennies spent much of their time rolling around on the floor, with parents hell-bent on retrieving them. On this occasion, the little rascal was throwing a Kellogg's Cornflakes packet on the ground so many times I became quite dizzy. "Hurry up Mummy. I'm really tired" I shouted, banging on the glass, as he giggled and chuckled non-stop.

The most vivid memories of my early education in County Down, were naughty boys messing up our skipping games, too much handwriting, huddling in the cold, sipping warm milk from tiny bottles and devouring our Janet and John reading books. Naturally John was peering under a car engine with daddy and the very docile Jill helping mummy with the washing up. One day in assembly I was chatting too much and had to sit in the corner for what seemed like ages. My cheeks stung with embarrassment as I took up the lonely position away from the rest of the class. After this occasion I was very careful not to be caught out again. Teachers on patrol were not to be messed with, when you were five and not yet six.

On our arrival home, I munched sweets and sucked on lovehearts while we enjoyed Watch with Mother, The Woodentops and Muffin the Mule. Funny puppets on strings, such as Bill and Ben the Flowerpot Men merrily danced across the grainy black and white screen and brought much delight. Little children were asked to peep through windows with the promise of magical stories beyond. There were nursery rhymes to recite and simple songs to clap your hands to. Perhaps, sitting cross-legged on the fireside rug with my blond pigtails and home-made jumpers, was the time when the seed of creativity was first sown. Before long my eager fingers were reaching out for a pack of crayons, a piece of paper and a sharpened pencil.

2

Under The Hen's Bottom

"Skedaddle! Shoo! Skedaddle!"

"Granny... Granny. I thought you'd never come back. I'm trapped in this tiny space. Can't breathe. Hurry up."

Granny shooed the quivering beast away from the corner of the Irish dresser, pivoting on the end of her sturdy brogues, with a pan lid in each hand.

"I was out feeding the pigs in the drizzle. They took their time wallowing. Then... I spent a while peering under Daisy's udder."

"Gran...nee...ee," I wailed. "Listen. I'm stuck."

"Now, what are you doing behind there? Squashed up so I can hardly see you. Of all the places to squeeze beside. I'm sure you were sitting at the kitchen table when I went into the yard. Neatly tucked in. Out of mischief... with your paper and pens writing the next masterpiece."

"I was reaching for something that rolled under the dresser. It slid off the table, bounced and flew right under here."

"Aah."

"I saw that thing... peering at me between the legs. Flying towards me. That horrible creature trapped me. Pecked my toes. Tried to kill me. Gobble me up. Trampled all over me." My soft Ulster voice grew harsh and shrill. Tears gathered in blue oval shaped eyes. Brown spindly legs were shaking.

"I said... skedaddle," she shouted, hands on hips, astonished at the barefaced cheek, the brazenness of the turkey, the audacity within.

It was loitering under the kitchen table now, glaring at the two of us, in no rush for the great outdoors. Planning the next move under the embroidered cloth with the frayed edges.

"Skedaddle. I don't know! Taking a risk. Dicing with death. Never

15

known anything like it. Shoo! Now, you come here Wendy. You've never heard of a human being killed by a turkey, have you?"

"No."

"Well then, give your old Granny a hug and let's have less of the imagination."

Her muscular arms opened like giant bellows releasing their power, slowly into the air. I sunk gratefully into the creased, cotton folds of the green floral pinafore. A smile returned to my pale cheeks as the round, comforting figure folded me between the smell of yesterday's rabbit's stew and the morning's warm Irish potato bread.

The red combed creature, with the quivering layers of black and white strutted over the flagstone floor. Tight, leathery, jagged claws scattered the dust. A head jerking from side to side as it pecked the mid morning air. In its own time. No rush. No need to hurry. I giggled, as an old stained table cloth was plucked from the washing basket and lassoed in the air, billowing above the head of the unwelcome creature. Soft worn brogues shuffled underneath, as her feet bounced on the floor and she hovered above the ground.

"I said shoo! The arrogance of that bird. If it's not careful we'll be having him for Christmas. Far too inquisitive for a life that's not its own. I think it waits until I've disappeared into the farmyard, then scuttles through the door. Cheeky thing! Now, dry those tears. Cheer up."

I pulled a face at the thought of the turkey on the large kitchen platter. The ugly beast, surrounded by little tatties and monster carrots. Aware now of the final warning, it took a flying leap out of the open kitchen door, squawking loudly.

"About time too! Don't be thinking about coming back in here," she shouted, as if it had been listening to our conversation.

"Now... don't be afraid Wendy of that old bird. Never show any fear. This is all part of life."

"Part of what, Granny?" I was curious.

"Life in the country. All the ups and downs. Every day is different. You never know what lies ahead. One moment your hand is sliding under a hen's bottom and the next minute you're delivering a slippery lamb in the early hours. I never thought I'd end up as a farmer's wife. I was living in the suburbs of a big city. Didn't know one end of a pig from another."

I giggled.

"When we first came to Hillside Cottage I caught my breath. It was so different to what I was used to. Jumping on trams. Lot of hustle and bustle."

"Aah… Granny."

"Your grandad came over her first Wendy. He used to fish on the banks of the river Bann. Every time he came back he was singing the praises of this little village. So we all travelled over lock stock and barrel."

"I didn't know that."

"And… gradually I got used to looking after all the animals, shoving the milk churns to the top of the lane for collection and feeding the chickens…"

"Do you like living here?"

"Well… yes… but sometimes it's very hard work. Do you understand where I'm coming from?"

"Yes."

I rested my blond plaits on her broad shoulders. I felt the warmth, the closeness, the smell of a caramel toffee on the breath, the taste of dandelion and burdock around her lips. A burst of rose scented cologne behind the thin grey hair on the nape of her neck.

"Just remember I love you," she whispered, kissing the middle bit of a flushed cheek and stroking my hair. "Sure… when you come to stay it's just the best. We both look forward to your visits in the school holidays. Life is always fun when you're here.

"And I love you too," I replied, holding her tightly around the waist so neither of us could breathe.

"Hmmm… now, tell me, what are you going to do next?"

"I might swing on the gate for a while… watch the steam train down in the valley… count the number of birds in the hedgerow searching for berries, and the cows in the opposite field. You can see the whole world if you stand at the top. It's my favourite place."

"Yes… but no falling off. No fancy manoeuvres. Your mummy and daddy would never forgive me. Remember the last time."

"I do."

"And in a short while… you must come and help me. It's a bit difficult on my own… especially today. So much to do."

"Not in the…"

"Yes. Now… no putting the moment off any longer… come on

17

Wendy. You're seven and a half and nearly eight. You'll be a great person to have around, now you're a big girl."

"Do I have to?" I pulled a face, starting at the top with a wrinkled brow, then a narrowing of blue eyes and a tiny mouth curled up into a tight red ball.

"Yes, you do. Your grandfather's not here today. He left early at the sound of the cockerel... when you were turning over. Tucked up in that warm bed, near the window, under the goose feather eiderdown with cosy feet. Did you hear him, or see his figure bobbing up and down the lane, having an early morning cigarette?"

"No I didn't. I was fast asleep," I answered, rushing outside, in my old jacket, only half listening to her idle chatter. I checked the turkey had vanished and the farmyard was relatively clear.

"Now come back in a while... no sneaking off."

"Yes... Okay."

Thirty minutes later, she lingered inside the open porch, gazing over at me practising a few cartwheels in the lane. Her eyes stared up inquisitively, at the dark clouds gathering in the sky, above the red tin roof with the tiny window in the eaves.

"Hurry up Wendy," she reminded me, "it's time, come on!"

We followed the path to the green corrugated building, past the straggly geese in the orchard. Wellington boots slid in the mud. A wicker basket swung on my fingers. White foxgloves and pink lupins scattered their moisture on my baggy shorts.

"I've told you before," Granny whispered, at the bottom of the slope. "Take a deep breath. Count to ten... slowly. Take your time Wendy. We've got all day. Place a hand gently under their bottoms and slide the eggs out. Don't look them in the eye."

"Yes Granny."

I knew she was right. She had been shoving hands underneath for years. She was still alive. There wasn't a hen celebrating in the corner. Her strategy was clear. It had never failed.

"Remember, they are more afraid of us than we are of them."

I nodded, as the image of the fat turkey running towards me returned. We stepped out of the persistent drizzle through the heavy door. My knees wobbled and wavered. There were hens everywhere. Newly disturbed. Several flapped in the air. One or two planned an escape route. Others sat on their nests, quietly squawking.

"Calm down girls," my grandmother whispered. "They will settle down in a minute. Always do. Know what to expect from me."

She squeezed my clammy hand and took the wicker basket. Our feet crunched on the brittle straw and hen droppings. I wavered near the entrance. Hesitating. Going over her simple instruction.

"Aah Wendy. Take that look off your face. You're a farmer's granddaughter from County Down. You've never heard of a human being killed by a chicken. Have you ever seen your grandfather pinned up against the wall?"

"No."

My throat was dry, lips tight. Feathers of red and orange missed my nose by half an inch. They changed perches and flew into the rafters screeching. I tried not to look at them or smell the unpleasant odour of the creatures.

Maybe Granny's magic had failed.

"Start counting now."

"1... 2... 3..."

The little bantam in front of me seemed strangely calm and peaceful. I felt so grateful.

"4... 5... 6..."

My right hand slid under the warm feathers and discoloured straw. The bemused hen moved over to the side. I held my breath.

"7... 8... 9... 10!"

Three brown, speckled eggs arrived between the fingers. Warm and delicate to touch. "Granny, Granny I've got three," I shouted, shaking the bounty.

"Well done! Magic. You're the best."

Heavy boots pushed the door open. The rain was still lashing down. A face appeared with cigarette breath and ruddy skin. My grandfather, in his Saturday best, was in a jubilant mood. He had purchased six new cows at the weekly cattle market and still had a pocketful of change. There would be good 'craic' in O'Callaghan's bar tonight. Granny and I might now have a peaceful evening, sharing stories and caramel toffees by the applewood fire.

"So how did she get on Ma? He gazed at my flushed cheeks.

"Our Wendy is a champion egg collector now. You're out of a job. I think she's cracked it... and even better she hasn't been killed by a chicken!"

19

My group of friends were swinging their legs on the low wall by the canteen. We chatted non-stop in our array of tartan skirts, homemade itchy jumpers or knitted cardigans. Unwelcome smells of washed-out cabbage and overcooked tapioca drifted in the air, reminding us of our forthcoming lunch that had to be eaten. The first few weeks of a new term at Primary School had passed by quickly. Friendships had been re-established. One or two of us felt a bit nauseous from the warm bottles of milk we had to drink every morning. Nobody was allowed to play until every drop had disappeared. The conversation, as usual, started like this. Competitiveness had crept in!

"I milked a cow at the weekend. It was so funny." Maggie spoke first. "My mummy said I was very clever."

"Well... I saw a piglet being born on Saturday morning," Lizzie told us.

"Yuck! I'm glad it wasn't me!"

"Well... I put my hand under a hen's bottom." I rose up in front of the others on tiptoe, hands on hips, shaking my pigtails.

"You didn't!"

"I did! It was the first time ever."

"I couldn't do that." Maggie was adamant. "Bet you didn't Wendy."

"I collected lots and lots of eggs in the henhouse. My granny said I was a champion egg collector... and no one got killed by a chicken."

"You're telling stories!"

"I'm not!"

"Bet you are."

3

Voulez-Vous

My grandmother leant forward and whispered softly in my ear, "Voulez-vous couchez avec moi ce soir mademoiselle ?"

"What does that mean Granny ?" I asked, curious for some kind of explanation.

"One day when you are older I will tell you." She sprang back in the chair with a mischievous smile, shelling the garden peas. One by one they bounced into the bowl, crashing against each other.

"But I'm seven and a half now Granny. I can't wait forever," I said, swirling my fingers inside and choosing one or two to nibble. Another school holiday had started. A glorious hot summer to pursue my imagination, in the fields and lanes around Hillside Cottage.

One late afternoon, my grandfather was in the farmhouse kitchen in County Down, with the flagstone floor and resident turkey. He was skinning a plump rabbit caught earlier for our Saturday night stew. I decided to seize another opportunity, as a pair of stubby fingers ripped off the pink moist skin.

"Voulez-vous couchez avec moi ce soir mademoiselle. What does that mean Grandad ?"

The beady eye of the dead creature on the slab gazed up waiting for the answer. The knife was suspended in mid air above the rabbit. Perhaps I had chosen the wrong moment.

"Hmmn... aah... well!"

"Well what Grandad ?"

"Well, just keep stirring the vegetables so they don't bubble over."

My grandmother had ambled down to the village shop, to pick up Woman's Weekly and her favourite caramel toffees. She used to call it the 'Grand Escape', where she met other escapees clutching brown

21

paper bags of sweets and rolled-up magazines. The sizzling air was hot with gossip and scandal. Children played in the sawdust and babies whimpered in their high carriage prams outside. If I was lucky, on her return there would be a sherbet fountain for me, or a liquorice wheel and she never ever forgot Grandad's pack of cigarettes.

Eventually childhood curiosity got the better of me. With no intention of being defeated, I felt the answer probably lay behind the frosty glass of the book cabinet. Here were rows of magical treasures, of different shapes and sizes. Some with gold writing and tiny black italics on their spines, to be taken out and admired. Wobbling on a milking stool, I opened the doors, trying to remember some of the words. At that moment, my love for the French language first began.

There was a growing fascination with the battered red French book on the third shelf. Written in the 1920s, it was full of faded drawings of naughty-looking Frenchmen and glamorous women with bright red lips. People loitering near the Eiffel Tower or perched on bicycles next to the river Seine. Stripy jumpers and twirling moustaches, strings of garlic and bottles of beaujolais. A fascinating world for someone seven and not yet eight.

"Who gave you that Granny?" I asked one evening. The sitting-room was cosy with the warm glow of the fire and the crackling logs from a fallen apple tree. There seemed a slight possibility that my questions might be answered. Granny had eaten more than half of her caramel toffees, so she was in a jubilant mood. Occasionally when she remembered, the paper bag was passed in my direction and I snatched as many as was possible."Well, as you keep asking, Wendy, I might just tell you tonight. It was a Frenchman!"

"A Frenchman?"

"I've had a colourful past," she whispered. "Sssh!"

"What do you mean? Have you? Which colours, red, green or blue?"

I tried to imagine a young woman sitting on a Frenchman's lap, just like the picture on page 62. Perhaps he had sung a song and told her she was beautiful. Her once black hair pinned up on top of the head. Smudgy bits of red lipstick were caught in the corner of the mouth. There was no sign of a floral pinny and a chicken under the armpit, but a silk lilac rose on a lapel and a whiff of perfume behind the ears."Of course... then I met your Grandad !"

"Are you filling that child's head with nonsense again Ma?" came a voice from behind. Grandad came into the sitting room smelling of cow manure and wet grass. He looked weary from an early morning start. Smudges of dirt were on his cheeks. "A Frenchman indeed! Whatever next?"

He pulled off muddy boots and placed them on the wide hearth, lit up his last woodbine and tossed the box into the flames. We watched it shrivel up with a vivid blue flame.

"Don't you listen to him Wendy. He doesn't know one half of it," Granny whispered, popping the last toffee into her mouth. "I could tell you some stories. Believe me."

Every evening before bedtime, when I came to stay in the school holidays, my grandmother carefully unplaited my blonde wavy hair. She wove her fingers in and out until the shimmering curls fell down the back, pulling and tugging at the scalp. The discomfort in my face was reflected in the dressing table mirror, but I never said a word.

"Aah... so lovely. It looks like the ripples of the sea at Donaghadee. I hope your mummy never cuts it. When I was your age, mine was the same but I couldn't wait to chop it off. Then I regretted it."

I was about to tell her that I longed to get rid of both plaits, so the rough boys at our primary school wouldn't pull them, but decided not to after all. She was too preoccupied with the hairbrush, the nightly ritual, and a chance to share fascinating stories of her childhood.

From when I was very young, Granny had sung the same line, "Voulez-vous couchez avec moi ce soir mademoiselle?" not expecting me to ever ask the question.

One night, she waved her arms around doing a funny dance on the kitchen floor, as she sang the words. Feet slid and slithered over the flagstones, arms waving in the air.

"Granny, you are the funniest person in the whole of County Down, but I still don't know what it means," I shrieked, as she nearly collapsed on her bottom.

"Well, now you are seven and nearly eight, I will tell you."

The moment had arrived. My blond hair touched the side of her warm face. She crouched down beside me, with caramel toffee breath.

"What is it then? Go on."

She stroked a hand as she spoke."Will... you sleep... with me... tonight... miss?"

The look of disappointment spread over my face. The frown

returned."...Is that it? Why would he want to sleep in your bed if you didn't know him? That's a wee bit cheeky," I said staring at the page.

"Just a little bit. He gave me the book before he went back to France."

"But... you still haven't told me. Did you sleep with him?" My curiosity wouldn't go away.

"Of course I didn't! Nice girls didn't!"

"Didn't what?"

"Didn't..."

"Are you still talking about that blessed Frenchman Ma?"

Neither of us had heard the return of Grandad's heavy boots on the floor. The latch was fastened and the rich velvet curtains pulled across."I think we should put that book back in the cabinet now don't you? We've had enough stories for one day. Whatever would your mummy say?"

He took the faded copy from my hands, gave a sigh and replaced it beside two other childhood favourites 'Little Women' and 'What Katie Did Next'.

But Granny's wonderful tale stayed with me forever. I remained unclear as to which grandparent was being truthful, but the thoughts fired my imagination and I chose to believe them.

~

A few years later September arrived again. The long hot summer soon forgotten, and the weeks spent at Hillside Cottage in County Down, chasing noisy turkeys, rolling milk churns and collecting eggs from under the hens' bottoms. This was my first term at secondary school. The excitement was unbearable. My father deposited me outside the gate in the old banger. I was dressed smartly in my navy and blue uniform and new squeaky shoes. Before lunch, we were sitting silently in neat rows in the language lab on the third floor. The first set of new pupils to benefit from the state of the art machines. My French lessons were about to start. I felt so happy, but there were no handsome Frenchmen and glamorous women in our books. Everyone looked very sensible, not a set of red lips in sight, or anyone peeping into a glass of Beaujolais. Our charismatic teacher introduced the first lesson.

"Bonjour mes enfants. Aujourd'hui c'est Lundi et c'est le Français. Eh bien... does anyone know any French words? Ah Wendy...?"

Lots of hands went up, but she chose me, as I bounced up and down on my seat.

"You are so keen. You are so enthusiastic. I like to see someone who likes the language. Tres bien."

"Voulez-vous couchez avec moi ce soir mademoiselle ?"

"Aah. Mon Dieu! Oh la! la!"

The rest of the class laughed at the sight of the French teacher clinging to her desk and clutching the text book, and at me with my innocent expression."Where did you learn that, ma petite?"

"My granny went out with a Frenchman, miss. That's what she told me."

Everyone chuckled.

"Non, Non, I am sure that is not true. Impossible! Your grandparents are dairy farmers in County Down n'est pas? How would she have met a Frenchman?"

"Well… she did Miss. My granny said she'd had a colourful past."

"What does it mean?" The girl opposite asked hopefully, longing to swop her sensible grandmother for mine.

"Something not for the ears of my French students. Now, no more questions mes enfants, let's look at page 10… tout de suite." She clapped her hands as we giggled and turned the pages.

"Spoil-sport," whispered the boy beside me. "I thought the lesson was about to get interesting. I hate French."

From that moment, on one autumnal morning in 1963, the teacher never took her eyes off the young pupil with the vivid imagination. I loved the language with a burning passion. When older I hoped to marry a Frenchman and live in Paris, which made all the adults giggle. Of course, I married an Englishman and never bought my dream flat near the Eiffel Tower or the Champs-Elysees.

One day many years later as a newly qualified teacher at a boys' secondary school, I hovered by the blackboard in front of the first set of French pupils.

"Did you really like French Miss?" the boy in the front row asked one morning. He had pulled many long faces since I had arrived that term. Languages were not on his agenda. I wondered if he might be my bête noir?

"Loved it," came the reply. "Don't know why. Just did."

I decided not to mention my grandmother's book, but smiled at the memory of my own 'little bit of mischief', in a faraway Ulster classroom.

"I'll never understand these words," said another, trying to make sense of the phrases in front of him. "Do we have to learn it? Why can't we go out and play football like that lot out there?"

"Yes you do, but let's make it as much fun as possible. Shall we?"

I spent my first few months after this promise, drawing '2CVs' and matchstick drawings of 'Jean-Paul est dans le jardin' on the blackboard. We acted out little plays that combined my love of drama with the French language. Soon lessons were full of twirling moustaches and stripy jumpers, as the children nose-dived off chairs pretending to buy baguettes and bottles of wine on the market stalls.

Their energy and enthusiasm was great fun, and at the end of the year I think they loved the language almost as much as me. All the boys perfected the greeting of 'Bonjour Monsieur' or 'Au Revoir Monsieur', every time the nervous Headteacher crept into the classroom. I was very proud of them.

4

Two Squares of Chocolate and a Floral Gazunda

I was ambling through the orchard one morning, followed by a hissing goose and a scraggy hen, when Grandad appeared from under a canopy of leaves. A man of few words. I knew something was up.

"Would you like me to make you a swing this morning Wendy?"

"Yes please." I jumped up and down on the earth with delight.

For the next hour or two I knelt beside him in my tatty red shorts and white t-shirt, watching his thick coarse fingers hammering nails into a piece of rough applewood. This had been lingering near an old milk churn for ages and would be ideal to make into a seat.

"That's what I call perfect. A dozen farmers could sit on that and it wouldn't break."

I giggled. My grandad pressed his hand firmly on the wood and I did the same. The other clear memory of that morning is the cigarette stub bobbing up and down on his lip, sending out little swirls of nicotine into the crisp September air. A source of much fascination.

"Now try it. Go on."

We were both anxious for success. I shuffled onto the rustic seat, hands clasping the knobbly rope either side. He watched while I gradually got faster and faster, swinging back and forth, further and further into the bushy trees.

"Now go easy," he shouted. "We don't want you disappearing over the henhouse, do we?"

I don't think anyone ever forgets the first moment they slither onto a swing. Magical and breathtaking are only two of the words to describe the occasion. As a child of seven and not quite eight I found myself transformed into a special world. From that moment writing stories took second place. Every morning in the school holidays I would dash through the yard, scattering chickens and dirt in a pair of red scuffed Clarks' sandals. I couldn't get there fast enough.

One lazy day, I heard my granny's sweet voice through the red shiny apples and thick foliage.

"Wendy... Wendy... your aunty's here."

"Yippee!" I shouted, jumping off the swing. How I adored her visits. Perched inside the doorway on a faded armchair, she wore a magnificent green and white polka dot dress. There she waited for her young niece, clutching both hands on her lap. I was about to dive into her bare arms, when the polka dots wobbled and wavered. The cotton material shook and shivered. Out popped three heads! My three little cousins, who had been hovering and waiting patiently underneath. I clapped my hands with glee and couldn't stop giggling as they dashed around the room with me in pursuit. At that moment at Hillside Cottage in County Down, amongst the merriment and laughter, I had never felt so happy.

Later that evening, Granny, sparkling with energy from her daughter's visit, hurtled around the warm kitchen pulling out drawers and peering into breakfast cups.

"Have you hidden my chocolate again?"

She was somersaulting into cupboards, pulling out bags of elastic bands, bits of string and old farm bills. I clapped my hands with joy, as she skidded on the flagstone floor, searching for the purple and silver foil. Spinning on the end of her carpet slippers, with me in tow, we dashed and zigzagged around the kitchen, until the search became unbearable.

"I must take after you Granny," I announced, as we hunted for the elusive bar.

"Well, that's not a bad thing." We both smiled at each other.

My bemused grandfather, in an old tweed jacket with fraying cuffs, loitered in the open doorway, smelling of a mixture of cow dung and knee deep grass.

"Now, come on, *where have you hidden the chocolate?*" I stood there, hands on hips, scrutinising his weathered country face, trying to emulate the posture of an adult. *"Tell us Grandad... please!"*

"All I need is chocolate!" Granny shrieked.

"Yes... all she needs is chocolate."

"Third drawer on the left Ma," he said eventually, wandering off into the yard past the squawking chickens and the newborn piglets. A whiff of nicotine mingled with the sweet smell of honeysuckle dangling outside the door.

"Here, come and share some of this Wendy," she whispered, as we both settled down on the red horsehair settee with the split down the middle. "I wish he wouldn't play tricks... don't you?"

The thick squares of chocolate were catapulted into her mouth one by one. I sat there in awe at such amazing powers. At that moment, I realised my granny's life often depended on the availability of the nearest chocolate bar. Every now and then, as the magic substance looked in danger of disappearing, she would remember her granddaughter. There I waited patiently, like an Irish Border collie with soulful eyes.

"Aah... sorry... here's one for you Wendy."

"Hmm," I said, licking my lips.

"Hmm," she replied, but even louder.

When our mouths were full of the chocolate liquid and our teeth the colour of rich mud, we would splash it down with the usual glass or two of dandelion and burdock. In the warmer months we sat on the steps, she and I, sipping the delicious liquid slowly, as the bees buzzed around the honeysuckle and rampant ivy dangled above our heads. My granny and I were very close. I was so fond of her I gave her a little hug. She stroked the top of my head and said quietly "I do love you. Especially when you come and stay."

"Love you too. You're the best granny in the whole of Northern Ireland with or without chocolate."

The other coveted items, often seen lingering in brown paper bags from the village sweet shop, were caramel toffees. My granny couldn't get enough of these and neither could I. My sweet consumption was very high as a child and eventually two teeth had to be removed prematurely when I was quite young, due to the overdose of sugar. Not an experience I wish to remember.

Eventually, my parents moved down into the village, from the tiny cottage, with an inglenook fireplace and outdoor privy, where they had started married life. In the new house, there was a wooden shack at the end of our rectangular garden which sold all kinds of sweets. Here inside were rows and rows of cluttered shelves, selling blackjacks, fruit salads, tubes of lovehearts and penny liquorice wheels. The ultimate experience all children craved in the 1950s, was the taste of a magical sherbet fountain. How could anyone resist these or anything else that lay inside those weathered timbers? On my own door step too. Perfect! Most days, I scuttled on my little red bike, in an attempt to be first in the queue. When the door was thrown open, the bigger kids rushed and clambered to get in front of us little'uns. Sometimes, we went unnoticed and had to stand back, as the older boys and girls snapped up all the goodies lingering in the glass jars. We watched in wonder, as fragrant smelling treats, such as pear drops, popped and fizzed inside their wide, grinning mouths.

One evening when staying at Hillside Cottage, as the gas lights were being lit, my grandmother unwrapped the biggest bar of chocolate I had ever seen. We sat there sprawled over the settee. The bright flames from the applewood fire were hissing and spitting.

"Granny?"

"Yes, love."

"Why do you keep chocolate by the bed?" I asked, as she clutched it between her warm fingers, like a small child she mustn't let out of sight.

"I can't go to sleep without this. One square or two... that usually does the trick," she said mischievously. "Just can't."

"But... I wish you wouldn't eat it when you're nodding off to sleep. I always think you are going to die."

"Now... don't be silly Wendy... As if I would. Put your books away now and no more nonsense. It's time for bed."

"But I do... I do."

We sauntered into the cosy bedroom with the sloping ceiling, for the regular bedtime ritual. *The brushing of the hair.* My blond plaits were undone and the ribbons put aside for another day. Granny's nimble fingers wove in and out, tugging and pulling as she moved down my hair. I pulled the usual faces and she gave a mischievous smile. There we relaxed, beside the dressing table with the pale green wallpaper above and the matching china dogs on the window sill. The heady smell of her favourite cologne was very comforting when you were only seven going on eight. I was balanced on a tiny stool swinging my spindly legs. Granny made huge sweeps with her soft hairbrush. Ripples of blond hair tumbled down my back, like the glittering River Bann dancing over the stones.

"Beautiful hair. Aah... such beautiful hair. Reminds me of my sisters. We used to sit and brush each other's hair before we went to bed... and tell stories to keep ourselves awake."

"What kind of stories Granny?" I was fascinated.

"Aah… that would be telling. We'd giggle and laugh for hours… until our ma would knock on the door and tell us to go to sleep."

"Did you take any notice?"

"No!" she whispered. "Not often."

"Sounds a lot of fun. I wish I had sisters, like you."

The bedtime ritual was always comforting. Just her and me and the stars shining through the gap in the cream curtains. The inky-black Ulster sky peeping in at the top. However… as I slid under the shivery cotton sheets in search of the hot water bottle… *I knew the second ritual was about to begin!* A hand reaching over in the semi-darkness… a rustling of purple and silver foil… fingers ripping open the wrapper… and the snapping of squares of chocolate. A popping in the mouth and a whizzing round and round… a crashing against the cheeks… and finally a noisy snore and a shudder! I leapt off my bed as usual, bouncing and skidding on the tiny bit of carpet between the two beds. My stomach was fluttering as I breathed in the thin cold air. I wasn't sure if I would get there in time.

"Granny… Granny are you still alive?" I shouted, shaking the white winceyette nightdress and the knobbly knees pointing up to the ceiling. *"Wake up! Wake up! Please! Are you still alive?"* I wailed.

There was a lot of grunting and muttering, as she turned over, before disappearing under several layers of blankets and an eiderdown. Then… an almighty snore and the strangest of sounds as she swallowed another piece. The remainder of the chocolate bar was snatched from the bedside table and stuffed under my pillow. I was now concerned with the task of weaning my granny from her nightly ritual. Would that be possible? At least I could sleep now. As I drifted off… I thanked God that her life had been saved and she would be still alive in the morning…

One late summer day in the school holidays, my grandad arrived home, with an unusual shaped parcel under his arm.

"What's that?" My curiosity emerged, as the package was poked and prodded.

"A gazunda."

"A what? What's a gazunda?"

"This thing in here." He plucked a white china pot with a handle on the side, out of the brown paper, like a magician dangling a white rabbit over a top hat. Pink blossom sprigs and clusters of leaves were sprawled over the surface. My eyes stared into the chasm.

"It's another name for a *po*," explained Granny whispering.

"Oh," I giggled, placing a hand to my mouth, on hearing the word.

"*Yes... a... gaz... un... da.*" Grandad was enjoying the sound of the rhythm, so he said it again.

"But... where do you put it?"

There was an explosion of laughter at my naivety .

"Just follow me and I'll show you." He tucked the object under his armpit and smiled. We traipsed in a straight line into the bedroom, hovering near the damp patch on the green wallpaper.

"Under here. It goes under here."

My grandad was enjoying the moment and wanted it to last for ever. So did I, even though I was still puzzled.

"This gazunda means your granny doesn't have to use the outside privy at night. When you go down those steps into the yard, there's lots of dark shadows and strange sounds out there. It's not very..."

"Hush. Don't frighten the child Pa. They're only foxes and passing badgers. Sure... you know that. Wendy's got a vivid imagination anyway. Don't make it worse."

Before I could ponder about the existence of wild scary beasts in County Down, Granny sprang into action. Never believing one should waste time, she dived onto the gazunda fully clothed. Her arms and hands fluttered in the air.

"Very easy to sit on. Look!" she shouted.

I giggled, jumping up and down at the figure sitting in front of me. Grandad didn't know whether to clap or not but I did. It was the funniest moment. There she wobbled in her dark blue dress and grubby pinny, pretending to do a demonstration.

Soon, my thoughts returned once more to bedtime. With her lack of co-ordination, would Granny take a flying leap in the middle of the night and knock the whole thing over? Something told me that I might never get any sleep again. Maybe even worse, the white winceyette-clad figure, devouring chocolate, would bounce off the bed springs, somersault and miss the gazunda altogether. How could her young granddaughter, on the opposite side of the room, ever hope to rescue her?

5

Passionate Loyalty

"Tidy your pigtails girls. Get those red ribbons straight. Tuck your shirts in boys. Gordon! Gordon! You're far too untidy. She can't possibly see you like that."

"Will she notice Gordon Miss?"

"Don't be silly, of course she'll notice Gordon. She'll have eyes for all of you. Pull them up child. Not down. And what are those things on the end of your feet?"

Miss Patterson, the class teacher was looking immaculate today in her royal blue knitted jumper, and a red tartan skirt with the sparkling gold pin. Once a month she asked for the latest hairstyle and we spent the whole of Monday morning breathing in the sweet, intoxicating fumes as she moved around the classroom with her correction pencil, the occasional hairgrip pinging on the floor.

"You don't need to pick them up Billy," she said in a half scolding voice. "There's hundreds of them holding up my bun. I won't miss one."

"Why does she call it a bun?" Maggie whispered. "That's something covered with jam and cream you eat. Nothing to do with the top of your head."

We all giggled, failing to appreciate the special perm which made the young teacher look like a starlet hovering on the front of a 1950s magazine.

"I can't stand the smell," said Lizzy in front of me. "It makes my nostrils twitch."

"It will be alright when we get out in the sunshine." I knew that we would all suffer, especially when Miss Patterson stopped to look at our work. Multiplication was not my strength so I always longed for the morning when we wrote our stories. If you struggled with sums like me, she lingered for longer periods, until the only escape was diving into your home-made school jumper pulling faces.

"Now," Miss Patterson paused for breath. "Have you all been to the toilet?" Those of us with an amazing bladder nodded and one or two pretended they had, shifting their feet under the desk.

"And you Andrew?"

All eyes turned to the shy, rather confused little boy, who had sat next to me since he had arrived at the start of term. A delightful soul who always looked as if he should be somewhere else, as if someone was going to collect him at any moment.

"Well... er... I think so Miss."

"Yes he did cos... he wet the floor."

"Gordon! Don't be so unkind."

"Sorry Miss."

One or two of the braver boys laughed as Andrew's eyes crumpled up.

"Dab your eyes." Miss Patterson removed a tissue kept cleverly tucked under her red belt for sad films and unexpected events, this being one of them, and thrust it into his hand.

"Now, now, now! We've all done that at some time, haven't we class?"

"Yes," came the chorus whether we had or we hadn't.

Andrew was clutching a large bright red and blue silk hanky which his English grandfather had given him for the special occasion. Half in and half out of his pocket, the intensity of the rich silk caught my eye.

The work in the classroom had come to a temporary halt. Miss Patterson, looking rather flushed and breathless, having deposited most of her hairgrips on children's desks, placed a picture face downwards, alongside a tiny new rubber and an unopened packet of colouring pencils, on every desk.

"For afterwards... and no peeping."

"It's a sort of surprise," Andrew whispered. "I wonder what it is?"

"Feels like someone's birthday," said Billy, but no one answered.

"Now everyone. The moment is here. So exciting." The teacher beamed and clapped her hands, spinning on her red shoes. "Everyone stand up."

Suddenly there was a mad scramble of arms and legs, white socks and sensible shoes. Bottoms bounced around as boys and girls hunted for floor space, pushing each other over and pulling hair. Those of us with long plaits like me didn't stand a chance. I gritted my teeth as two separate hands yanked them.

"They're mine."

"No they're mine."

"Where's my shoelaces? Miss, he's taken my shoelaces."

"I'm sure she won't be looking at our feet, will she Miss?"

In the frantic fight for survival Andrew nearly lost his red and blue silk hanky. Determined to keep it safe, his grubby fingers pushed it as far as he could down into the bottom of his pocket.

"Now children. Behave!"

The effect was immediate. Everyone doing something they shouldn't, no matter how trivial, stopped immediately. Who needed a megaphone when your teacher was Miss Patterson?

"In twos please! In twos. Can't you count? Gordon, Lizzie, Wendy, Billy."

We all grabbed the nearest hand and formed a quiet queue as we meandered out of the red hot stifling classroom. The cupboard outside P3 was flung open and there they were. From the deepest box we had ever seen, the teacher, without ruining the new hairstyle, or moving that tissue from under her belt, handed each of us a Union Jack flag. A few gasps echoed in the corridor, as this was the first time some of us had ever held one.

"You match the flags Miss." Billy was feeling brave.

Miss Patterson grinned and patted him on the shoulder. "Thank you."

It was as if Cary Grant, her idol, had suddenly found her a part in his new play. We had never seen her look so animated the whole term.

"Och children. I did say, ask your mummies and daddies to choose red, white or blue today, when you got dressed. Of course... some of you weren't able to do so... well never mind! However, one or two of you might have gone a little bit over the top. Now children, we must try and do our bit for Queen and Country. After all none of the Catholic children will be in the slightest bit interested. We're so lucky, it's not every day that she..." and out slid that tissue again.

It wasn't long before the excitement and fervour of the occasion took over. Some of the boys started waving their flags a bit too enthusiastically and of course the more boisterous ones turned theirs into flying weapons, jabbing nostrils and detaching ribbons.

"Class!"

The voice was enough to knock you sideways, make you shake in your guttees!

"Now! Follow me."

With thumping hearts and clammy hands attached to other clammy hands, we moved out into the bright sunshine, shuffling past the children from other classes. The fierce heat of the afternoon circled above our heads, and we envied those wearing sunhats. Red, blue and white triangular bunting fluttered from the black gates of our Northern Ireland Primary school. A tall, austere cream building with high windows and a stone yard at the back. From the shops and offices opposite, people streamed out, lining the pavements with their homemade flags and passionate loyalty.

"This way Class 3. This way."

We had been given a special area in front of the black school gates. The smaller ones, including Andrew and me, stood at the front and the taller ones at the back, prodding and poking when Miss Patterson wasn't looking.

"Don't wave your flags yet children. You'll use all your energy and then when she comes round the corner it will be *so disappointing*. Keep them down by your side."

"Miss, Miss, Andrew's lucky Miss. He's got a red and blue hanky and a Union Jack flag."

I clutched his hand tightly and watched the silk handkerchief slide out of his other pocket, like a magician who'd come to spend the afternoon in class. Andrew gazed at it for a moment.

"Do you?" he asked.

I nodded. "Yes please."

He handed it over slowly. With sheer pleasure I touched the silk, it was soft and beautiful. My fingers glided over the fabric.

"You have this then."

"Thank you." It was an easy swap.

The moment had arrived. This was it. I shook the red and blue shimmering silk. He waved the two flags as fast as he could. Here was the main purpose of the whole week, not just that day. For Miss Patterson our lively teacher, the purpose of her whole life, being an avid royalist. In the distance, from the left, shimmering in the heat was the black limousine, creeping nearer and nearer to the buzz of the waiting crowds. Miss Patterson, who despite being five feet nine inches tall was at the front, in the best spot, bounced up and down like a pogo stick. Her arms waved madly in the air and she was shaking three flags. It hardly seemed fair. Tears of excitement fell down her cheeks; it was as if her movie idol had spotted the attractive creature in the crowd.

"WAVE CHILDREN. WAVE CHILDREN." The words bounced off the school building. We leapt up and down finding that last bit of energy from somewhere. The people opposite chanted her name. 'Queen Mum, Queen Mum.'

Around the corner came the black car and there she was. Magical. An admiring hush went through the throng. The morning's intense activity had been worth it. The Queen Mother in pale blue with a set of cream pearls smiled over, first to the right and then to the left. She waved her hand in tiny circles, and every member of our class waved back, pushing forward to get a closer view. Andrew in all his excitement found his feet whirling dangerously on the edge of the pavement in his white guttees. He had lost one of the flags. I shook the red and blue hanky until my hand nearly parted from my wrist. Andrew didn't mind at all. He was perfectly happy with the remaining Union flag.

"Don't stop waving." Miss Patterson was quite delirious.

"But my hand's killing me Miss."

"Mine's snapped in two."

The other teachers were screeching as much as we were. I felt I was going to burst.

Slowly in small groups, the people opposite dispersed with shiny red faces, and smiles. The car disappeared further and further down the street. Soon, only the number plate was slightly visible in the hazy heat, until the letters had vanished completely. We hesitated for a moment, waiting for instruction, not quite sure what to do next.

"Come on children, follow me."

With flags down by our sides we turned, clutching a different clammy hand from the one we came out with. Slowly, all the children ambled back into the classroom, some trying to find a bit of mischief on the way. The teacher's perm had collapsed in the heat and her cheeks were scarlet... but her eyes were full of joy.

"Is that it Miss? Will she be coming back?"

"Where is she going now?" We all spoke at once, not wanting to return to the dark classroom with the high windows.

"Yes children. The visit's over but didn't she look beautiful? Now...

sit down… sensibly. But… don't lose faith… it's not finished yet."

A few faces including mine took on a hopeful expression.

"Now, turn your picture over." We did so obediently, staring at the face on the other side. "The child who uses their imagination the most creatively when colouring in the Queen Mother gets a prize at the end of the afternoon. And, don't go over the edges."

"It doesn't really look like the face we saw in the car Miss." Gordon held the piece of paper in front of him scrutinising the smile. We exchanged glances and no one said a word. Miss Patterson came round and collected the flags one by one.

"Do you think she saw all of us Miss?" asked Lizzie, as she tried to decide the best way to colour in the pearls. "I think she looked at me first."

"No, she looked at me the most."

"Do you think the Queen Mother noticed your new hairstyle Miss?" Billy felt compelled to ask. All the boys giggled. A whiff of special perm had passed his shoulder. Miss Patterson grinned, patting the remains of the original creation.

"I think she noticed Andrew," I said confidently. "He was the first person she saw when the car turned the corner."

The shy boy, who had sat quietly next to me for half a term, didn't look up. He was too busy! He was on a mission, hopefully heading for success. His colouring pencils flew across the picture. Without hesitation, Andrew knew exactly how to capture the softness in the eyes and the colour of her lips. The other children around him were dropping items off the desk. Someone got upset because a hole had appeared on the page. I felt annoyed because I had used the wrong colour for her hair and now had to change it. With a renewed air of confidence, Andrew put his last crayon down and waved the finished item in the air.

"Miss, Miss," he shouted, almost exploding. "Finished."

"Well, what a miracle. Quite perfect. You really were paying attention Andrew. Now everyone else… there's plenty of time, no need to hurry, children."

"Do you think she'll come in and collect the pictures?" I asked hopefully.

"Maybe one day Wendy… maybe…"

"Bet she doesn't," said Gordon, putting the finishing touches to the Queen Mother's cheeks. After all the excitement and activity he hoped, as we all did, that he might be rewarded with the 1s/6d... the first prize.

The Queen Mother never returned to see such colourful masterpieces from Ulster's budding artists. Eventually after a couple of weeks on the wall, no one, not even Andrew, the winner, mentioned her again.

6

The Russian Princess

The loose floorboards, old and thin, squeaked in the attic above my head, as Grandad moved across them. I pictured him, splashing ice-cold water on his sallow skin and shaving... scraping the blade slowly... precisely... over the grey stubble. The discoloured suds swirling in an oval bowl with a frayed flannel. Braces dangling on either side of the hips, as he stood there weary from a long journey. A cigarette maybe... waiting to be lit, balanced on the narrow attic window-sill, and a battered leather suitcase open on the iron bed, with crumpled shirts and trousers inside.

Beyond the tiny panes of fragile glass, my grandfather would often gaze at the scuttling ducks weaving in and out of the farmyard. I noticed a tall skinny figure sometimes, staring out at his domain, while I negotiated a safe path, past the creatures that nipped or spat at me on the way to the orchard swing.

"Do you think Grandad will be down soon?" I asked, shoving thick chunks of Irish wheaten bread with dripping butter, into my hungry mouth.

"Manners," said my granny watching the crumbs scatter. "He'll come down those stairs when he's ready and not before."

In the middle of the scratched oak table, amongst the breakfast dishes and the tiny posy of buttercups, lay a crumpled up parcel in brown wrapping paper. It rose above the white crockery with the thin gold rim and the plates of steaming soda farls... a splendid package, tied with thick red string.

"I wish I could open it now Granny."

"Be patient," she said. "Think how we will enjoy the surprise when he says we can."

My grandmother threw the door open to allow the summer air to filter in. It was the start of another delightful school holiday. A strong scent of madonna lilies and purple delphiniums filled the room. Clusters of frilly-edged clouds hovered in the deep blue sky above. The skinny-necked geese with their bright yellow beaks delivered their high pitched sound, as they congregated at the top of Drumiller Lane. Granny's daily ritual of shooing away the arrogant cockerel always made me giggle. She had perfected the art of its departure with great panache. She rose above the flagstones with a determined expression, spinning on her old slippers and shaking the pinny at the strutting beast. As usual, it examined her grinning face for a few seconds, before deciding it preferred the great outdoors. I listened to the familiar sounds of the squawking hens nearby with their quivering orange-red feathers, pecking in the dusty earth and fighting over the soda bread crumbs.

"*Your grandfather is late,*" she said, scrutinising the creaking floor boards. What is he doing? I've got to stick a hand under a hen's bottom and examine Daisy's udders before eleven thirty."

I giggled at the thought of her chasing the chickens and tussling in the byre with the ancient cow.

"I'll help to collect the eggs today," I said with a new-found confidence. My previous fears of those fluttering creatures had long since gone. However, it was extremely unlikely that even at the age of nine and three quarters, I would ever stick my hand around a cow's udder.

Before long he appeared at the bottom of the attic stairs smiling. "Grandad," I yelled, scurrying towards him.

"Ah, it's great to be home again. Morning Ma."

I was lifted up and spun round in the air, a cigarette dangling on his lip, puffs of smoke circling the pair of us. Granny fluttered nearby in her fresh green pinny, with a lingering whiff of floral scent.

"You were back late last night."

"Yes."

"I heard the latch and the dog growling."

"The boat was very slow and the train delayed."

"Ah."

"Where have you been Grandad? I've missed you."

"Russia."

"Where's that? Is it near Northern Ireland?"

"No, it's a long way over the sea," he replied, as my grandmother filled his mug up with strong orange-coloured tea. The liquid splashed over the edges as she plonked the enamel mug down beside him.

"Why did you go there?"

"Precisely," said Granny waiting for a reply.

"Russia's a great place. Marvellous to visit. So different from here."

"A long three weeks," she muttered, gathering up the dishes.

"Yes, but why did you go there?"

"Because he's a communist."

"What's that?" I was more puzzled than ever, as a tiny piece of my magical world crumbled at the edge. "I thought you were a dairy farmer in County Down."

"Yes I am," he said, enjoying the banter and a chance to be mysterious.

"Will you be going again Grandad?" We drifted in front of him waiting for an answer. I was more curious than ever.

"The first of many visits I hope," he said, slurping mouthfuls of the hot sweet liquid. "Now no more questions. I have a little something for you both. I think you will be delighted."

Being easily distracted, I clapped my hands and turned my attention to the oblong parcel on the table.

"Wendy's waited all morning. She's been very patient," Granny told him. She winked at me and I nodded back.

"Well here you are." He leant forward and grabbed the package.

My eyes sparkled with anticipation, as she clutched her gnarled hands together. We both tried to imagine what treasures could possibly be inside.

"A little something all the way from Moscow."

"Moscow! I've never heard of that place. Is it like Belfast?"

"No."

Granny slid a chair closer to the table. She beamed with delight as my nimble fingers clutched the presents, shaking and squeezing them for any vital clues.

"Go on then. Stop teasing us. I haven't got all day. Daisy's waiting!"

Her warm soda bread breath was blowing on my face and the blue glittering eyes keen and focused. I undid the thick red string and ripped off the brown paper, faster than I ever thought possible. Inside were two parcels nestling in white tissue.

"Yours is the smaller one Wendy," Grandad pointed out, as he sat upright in the chair delighting in the spectacle. "Hope you like it. There won't be another one in Northern Ireland."

Out of the paper folds popped a Russian toy soldier perched upright on his horse. I held him up between the three of us, fascinated, twirling him round and round in the mid-morning light.

"Aah... he's lovely. I've never seen anything like this," I said, clutching the red and yellow tin soldier with the tiny set of black drums.

"I knew you would like it."

I rushed over and planted a kiss on his rough wrinkled skin, breathing in the smell of the strong nicotine breath and the green carbolic soap on each cheek.

"Thank you," he smiled, fiddling with his braces. "That makes me very happy."

"So what does he do?" My curious grandmother was bouncing up and down like a carefree child on a garden trampoline.

A silver key slotted into the side. I twisted it until the drums exploded into action. The tin soldier seemed to grin as I lowered him down onto the flagstone floor. Off he went... *whirring and banging...* like a giant hiccup when he hit the cracks... *moving and shaking...* as he gathered speed. The breakfast crumbs near the cream Aga scattered, and a scraggy hen peeped through the open door, before dashing away to join the others. Brahma, the border collie, growled quietly but kept his distance, as I snatched the soldier up again, to restart the action.

"It's the best thing. I'll treasure him forever."

"I bought him in a Russian toy shop."

"Really?" My eyes sparkled as I clutched the soldier, worried that someone might snatch him at any moment.

"Now Ma it's your turn. Go on." Grandad settled back in the chair lighting up another cigarette.

Granny lifted the black furry object up in both hands. There was no disguising her delight or mine.

"Is it alive Grandad?"

"No, don't be silly."

"Is it an animal?" I couldn't imagine Granny standing there with a beast wrapped around her grey curls.

"Of course not."

I stroked the dark and shimmering fur. It was warm and soft to touch and made my fingers tingle.

"Aah," she muttered. "Now, what do you do with it?"

He rushed over, scattering the cigarette ash on his khaki trousers. "Stand still... now put it on your head Ma. All the ladies wear them in Russia because it's so cold. No... like this... not like that. Oh dear... where have you gone?"

I jumped up and down in delight as Granny disappeared under the hat chuckling, her face obliterated by the thick fur. The muffled voice tried to escape as she waved her hands around. Grandad smirked, replacing the hat at the right angle.

"It's a Cossack hat. They keep you lovely and warm. Their winters are very harsh over there. Will be a good thing to wear on the farm when the weather changes."

I gazed up at his animated face. "One day... will you tell me why you go there Grandad? Please?" I asked, remembering he had never answered.

"Aah... hmn... that's a question for another time. Now... let's look at the Russian Princess standing in front of us. Have you ever seen such a...?"

We both stood back circling around her with admiration. Granny gazed into the mirror on the wall near the open window, pulling faces and quietly admiring herself. Our reflections were caught behind her shoulder in the tarnished glass.

"Now what do you think Ma? Wendy?"

My grandmother twirled back and forth with flapping arms. She clutched her pinny, the blue crepe dress underneath swishing and swirling above the broderie anglaise petticoat, as she swayed from side to side. A simple row of pearls bobbed up and down on her pale neck, peeping above the sweetheart neckline.

"Doesn't really match the old slippers," she said skidding to a halt. Without any warning my granny swept me up and pulled me towards her. Coarse fingers dug into my tiny waist, as I flew up into the air.

"Let's dance. Let's dance," she shouted. "Come on."

We spun over the uneven flagstone floor, past the rabbit stew bubbling in the pot and the overflowing vase of pink lupins and white aquilegia. Up and down the kitchen and round the table we skipped, over the breadcrumbs and past the startled Brahma. Grandad jumped up, stamping his battered leather boots and clapping hands to the rhythm.

Faster and faster we moved, until my feet hardly touched the ground. Twirling this way and that, I winced as her fingers clung on to my red cotton waist band, digging into the flesh.

"Granny... Granny...! I've got no breath left. *I'm dizzy.* Stop... stop... please," I spluttered.

We crumpled on top of each other in the middle of the old settee. Hardly able to whisper. Arms and legs akimbo. Flashes of red, blue and cream above the faded leather. The blast of heat from the old Aga blew across our faces.

"Well, wasn't that the best sight I've ever seen in County Down," said Grandad.

He hovered above with folded arms, as the Cossack hat shimmered between us. I lay beside my grandmother as we tried to lift ourselves up. Damp hair was sticking to our flushed cheeks, as we looked for somewhere to wipe clammy fingers.

"Aah Granny... you are the most beautiful princess in the whole of Ireland," I whispered, as we slowly got our breath back.

"And the whole of Russia," Grandad reminded us.

"Thank you. I've never had so much fun. Such a wonderful gift." Grandma placed the quivering fur hat back on her head. "Oh dear," she suddenly shouted, springing to her feet. "It's eleven thirty and I've forgotten all about Daisy... her poor udders... I'll be back in a moment." She grabbed a bucket and some rubber gloves and leapt through the door in her beige carpet slippers. The creatures outside scattered. Grandad and I couldn't stop laughing at the mad dash into the farmyard.

From that moment on, the Cossack hat accompanied my grandmother everywhere. On the hottest of days or the coldest it made no difference. Often, she popped it on her curly hair when feeding the chickens, a source of great amusement in the henhouse, or sometimes when sweeping the messy farmyard, with me in tow. My Russian soldier was constantly whirring around the kitchen floor, until one day sadly I lost the key. Despite scouring every nook and cranny we never found it, but the source of such joy still lies in a box of childhood memories.

My paternal grandfather often visited Russia, yet I never found out why. There were occasions when I caught enticing snippets, tales of his exploits from whispering adults who came to visit. Once he was arrested for tossing a cigarette butt on the pavement. On another intriguing occasion, he cracked a rib and ended up in a Russian hospital.

So, to start with I thought it was best to keep the mystery of his solo travels and zany adventures to myself. So no one at school ever had the slightest inkling that my charming grandmother was really a Russian Princess and my eccentric grandfather a secret communist.

7

An Honorary Catholic

Our house at number 27 was at the end of the street, just past the dip on the left and a turning off to the right. There was a shedding pink magnolia tree and a shabby Ford Prefect parked badly in the drive. Life at number 25 however, seemed more enticing, so I spent as much of my time there as I could. There were four boys next door and many toys to play with. We rushed up and down the road on our noisy scooters and took part in skipping games with funny rhymes. Scraped our knees and shared the bruises.

One July morning we were gathered in the Mulligans' cramped hallway. There was a feeling of anticipation, and the delightful smell of early morning baking. We children looked from one to the other. Peter the eldest seemed to know something we didn't. There we lingered, waiting for further instructions, in our scruffy tee shirts and faded summer shorts. Tightly packed and a bit of a squeeze. Tuesday morning at ten thirty.

"Christy bought this yesterday," Mrs Mulligan said proudly. "A great bargain, right at the back of the shelf. The last one. Mrs O'Reilly had her eyes on it but he got there first." She held up a brown paper bag. "They've been very popular Wendy. There was a bit of a queue, and now here it is. Imagine that."

I wondered what might have been so important, to have made their easygoing father forget his manners when he nudged the lady from number 7 out of the way.

"I was with Daddy," Peter said. "Mummy thought we needed a new one and Mrs O'Reilly didn't really mind."

"What is it?" The excitement for me was unbearable. Why couldn't someone take out the contents and put us out of our misery? We huddled together staring at the special package.

Marie Mulligan, with cheeks like the red flush of an early apple, fluttered like a lively moth in search of a light. There she drifted, glowing in a tight blue dress, arms folded. The harsh colour made my eyes sting, as her hand dived into the bag. "Look at this everyone," she shouted, swinging it in front of our noses. "What do you think boys?"

The new font, cream with a picture of Jesus and Mary emblazoned at the top, popped out. "Our old one had a leak. Took the colour out of the carpet where they stood and splashed themselves. We had to replace it Wendy."

"Where was it?"

"Upstairs on the landing outside the bathroom."

I tried to imagine what their house was like upstairs, because in those days one never went further than the hall.

Having to splash yourself every day was quite intriguing and sounded hard work to me. I had never witnessed this strange event, as my parents were non-believers.

"You fill this bit up with Holy Water," Mr Mulligan explained.

"And you have to fill it back up when it gets empty," said John.

"Oh!"

"And you mustn't splash your clothes either or you'll be told off. We have to bless ourselves every day and think about Jesus and the Virgin Mary."

"And the Pope," Sean whispered in a hushed tone. "Then we can do what we like afterwards."

"Sean… where did you get that idea from? Don't let the Holy Father hear you say that."

The youngest boy was suitably chastised and silenced. Mrs Mulligan looked up and crossed herself and we did the same. "He doesn't miss anything. Remember!"

"Will we ever get to see him Mummy?"

"No, he keeps himself tucked away John. I don't think so."

"Oh, that's a pity."

Everyone was restless. Too much religious fervour might not always be good for the soul. It was a fine day and there was a longing to be outside with the crowd. But we all knew better than that. There was a kind of understanding… that no one could rush off into the sunshine yet, until their mother had exerted her usual authority.

"So much bigger than our last one." Christy Mulligan held the font up in one hand, a hammer and hook in the other. "And it's just perfect."

"Yes!" I stared at the object that might soon be dangling on the wall at the bottom of the stairs. Jesus had a kind smile and the Virgin Mary was staring up with adoration.

"I wish we could have one of those," I said wistfully.

"You're not a Catholic," Peter reminded me.

"Aah... come on boys... our Wendy's an Honorary Catholic. We'll have none of that. Now, you come over here."

"Thank you Mrs Mulligan."

Their kind mother curled her arm around my shoulder and gave me a tight squeeze. I wasn't sure of the meaning... but how good to be included, to be part of this vibrant family, whose feet clattered on the pavement on their way to Mass every Sunday morning. Every time I heard their laughter though, I slid down into the bath water, shutting out the sound of the church bells. They never knew and I would never tell them. Religion was very low profile in our house.

I imagined the scene later that night. We would be perched round the table after tea. There might be a pause in the conversation, while my father lit up the final cigarette of the evening. And then the question would leave my lips before I had time to regret it. His answer direct and simple.

"Well, I shall have a word with those Mulligans. No daughter of mine is taking part in a ritual involving Holy Water and a font. It's bad enough the local vicar always wants to save your soul."

Mr Mulligan was anxious to return to his beloved garden and the untangling of the sweet peas, but he tried to stay as patient as possible. This was a day off, the first one for ages and he longed to be outside, with fresh soil on his boots and a trowel in his pocket.

"Where shall we put it then Marie?" He turned and winked at us all. Our eyes focused on his animated wife. No one dared breathe.

"I'll just take a minute," she said. "It's a big decision Christy. Don't rush me."

"I'm not."

We waited patiently for the answer. Stood there silently. Looked from one to the other, the piercing sounds of the rowdy street in our ears, the fragrant scent of the penny sweets in our pockets. She moved off to the left, then to the right, peered up the stairs and then down. Stood spinning on one leg in her shabby carpet slippers. Leant against the wall with a finger pointing upwards. We could hear the rapid breathing in her chest and smell the whiff of lavender cologne. My heart was quivering as I found myself caught up in the religious fervour.

"Come on Mummy," shouted Peter.

"Hurry up," said Sean, bouncing up and down.

"Hmm…" she said. "Well…"

"Are you okay Mrs Mulligan?"

"Grand," she whispered, "just grand Wendy. You can't rush these moments."

We were all glued together now at the bottom of the stairs. On the faded part of the carpet where a pale pink rose met a twisting leaf. The hall was hot and humid with a lack of air.

"There," she shouted at last. "Over there Christy."

"Aaah," her husband's face swivelled round. How did she think he… perhaps if he stretched or stood on tiptoe… took a chance. It was possible that he could…

"That's too high for us little'uns Mummy," said Sean, as their father teetered and reached up, in his baggy garden trousers and open necked shirt.

We tried not to giggle. His mother in the soft swishy dress was leaping around doing a version of an Irish dance.

I was captivated. One by one we stood back, waiting calmly in the steady stream of sunlight from the glass front door. Diamond patterns glittered on the hall carpet and over our bare feet.

"Well… er… how about there?"

Mr Mulligan, who had the patience of his favourite saint, didn't move, waited for a few seconds in case Marie changed her mind again. He was poised, hammer and font in hand, ready for action.

"Stand back children," he grinned. "This is our big moment."

His wife clung on to the banister staring at the chosen place.

"Get the angle right Christy," she reminded him. "I can't bear new holes in the wallpaper."

We placed our fingers in our ears even though we didn't need to. There was very little noise, a kind of a squeak, a mild explosion. Everything was fine. The perfect place. Jesus and Mary resplendent in their bright colours peeping down. They were up on the wall at just the right angle.

"It doesn't even need rearranging," she told us, with a smile. Unlike her husband who had needed a lifetime of rearranging.

"Well done Christy. Perfect. Thank you." She kissed the dark red cheeks and hugged him until he begged to be released. We chuckled at his beetroot-coloured face.

"I'll get the new bottle of Holy Water." Peter rushed off, into the galley kitchen. He liked to think he was in charge.

"Watch the carpet son," said Mr Mulligan. "Please... don't trip."

The enamel jug was full and the contents were swaying from side to side. Peter moved deliberately across the hall. Everyone went quiet as the water slid in. The three boys knew what was expected of them. Their main thought now was to get the ceremony over as soon as possible. The outside was beckoning. Fierce slithers of morning sun peered through the hall window, past the coat stand and the collection of shoes on the carpet. Jesus was bathed in light. Their mother was right; the colours were soft and muted, gentle and calm, quite beautiful. He seemed to gaze on them with approval, pleased the right amount of time had been spent on his elevation.

"Aah... it looks lovely there," I whispered, and she smiled back, enjoying the female approval.

"Now line up. Behave, boys. One at a time. No shoving and pushing."

Marie lingered close by her offspring, a fresh tissue clasped in the hand. Holy water tumbled from the end of their fingers as the sign of a cross was made.

"Mrs Mulligan?"

"Yes love!"

"Do you think I could...?"

"I don't see why not Wendy, as you are an Honorary Catholic. Leave some for her boys. Move over."

I wiped my hands over the green cotton shorts, creeping slowly towards the font, while the others stepped aside. John pulled a face and Peter grinned. Their parents stood poised, arms round each other. A relief! Each son was now suitably soaked and blessed. Now, it was the turn of the young girl next door. My fingers fell into the font, enjoying the cool liquid. The Virgin Mary beamed down. I made a cross on my forehead encouraged by the boys' mother, who was nodding like a cute puppy dog in the back window of a Ford Prefect. A drop of liquid trickled down the nose and brushed my lips. The taste was cold and salty

51

on the tip of the tongue. With amazing agility, she was there once more, to catch the water with the remains of a tissue. Her slippers skidded on the carpet.

"Bless the Pope and all of us," she whispered, "but don't tell your mummy and daddy, as they might not approve."

"Or that you're an Honorary Catholic," added Mr Mulligan. "You don't know what they might think. Best to keep it a secret."

"Yes."

"You don't have to splash yourself again unless you want to. He won't mind."

I looked up at Jesus half expecting a response, some sign of disapproval, for someone who had never been inside a church.

"Lucky you Wendy," said Peter realising the importance of only being an honorary something. "We'll have to do it every day now."

"And twice on Sundays," his mother reminded him before he disappeared.

The other boys had flung open the front door. The light was flooding in. Now the ceremony was over, we would be given permission to rush outside into the hot midday sun. Other people's children were screaming and shouting. A game of hopscotch was under way. The pecking order had been established.

The pale pink magnolia tree in our front drive had shed more of its blossom on the tarmac, and my father had re-parked the Ford Prefect in the road. He loitered under the branches in a white singlet, a cigarette dangling on the end of his lip, watching my mother tending the summer flower bed. Mr Mulligan would soon be untangling the sweet peas, and banging stakes into the earth. His wife peeping out of the window, showing her appreciation for the dazzling colours chosen this year.

At that particular moment, there was more to life than being an Honorary Catholic. After all I was only nine going on ten. There had been enough religion for one day. I raced out into the street in search of a new adventure.

8

Red Sandal in the Bog

Outside in the pink early morning sun, the magnolia tree was in full bloom. The palest of delicate blossoms tumbling on the Ford Prefect roof and windscreen. A petal storm scattering above the tarmac.

My father hovered in the doorway with nicotine breath and a white singlet. Thin and slim, with slicked-back hair, baggy trousers and brown boots of soft worn leather. "This idea is the best one yet," he said, tossing a cigarette butt into the rose bed.

"Yeah… but is it going to make us rich?" I was dancing around the drive in a new pair of red sandals, as my mother gazed over at me. "So… you go with your daddy to keep him company today. You don't see him very often and I've got a lot to do."

"But I'd rather stay here Mummy. *Please.*"

The boot was wide open. A pickaxe, shovel and hessian sacks crammed inside, on top of old newspaper.

"What does he need all those for?" I watched my parents darting from the house to the car, my head stuck in the boot, pressed up against the side.

"Ask him, not me," she said.

"Daddy?"

"Well… I'll see you later love. Not sure what time we'll be home."

"Okay." My mother waved, perched beside the open glass door, arms folded, in green cotton. I blew her a kiss.

"Where *are* we going? Tell me."

"Jump in and we'll talk in the car. Must get a move on, or I've wasted my day off. It's ten o'clock. Hurry up Wendy, it's a bit of a drive to the Derry bogs."

"Why are we going there…? I don't understand."

The sleek Ford Prefect reversed slowly into the road through the black gates. A few children interrupted their game of hopscotch, peering in and pulling faces. Billy McVeigh at number fifteen stuck his tongue out. I twisted round and did the same. My father beeped the horn and everyone dispersed like the slippery blossom on the front drive.

"I wish they would chalk on someone else's bit of pavement," he muttered, as we pulled out of our road.

"What's Mummy going to do?" I was so used to her company, and here I was plonked on the leather seat next to a zealous father. My spindly legs in the shiny red sandals dangled over the edge.

"She'll be busy as usual. A chance to have a cuppa with the neighbours. Have a bit of a break."

I imagined my mother sipping tea, under the picture of the Pope with Mrs Mulligan, or maybe choosing to spend the time with Mrs Smart our other neighbour and the newly framed photograph of Ian Paisley.

"Do you think she'll miss us?"

"Not one bit." He laughed at the thought of it. "Now, don't sulk. Look out of the window. Help me follow the signposts."

The children outside our sitting room window might be in the middle of another game of hopscotch now. Hopping and leaping, spinning and turning, sprinkling the chalk as their feet tried to land between the squares. Pushing each other over. Giggling and squabbling as they collected fresh bruises. I wondered what questions they might ask me tomorrow.

We stopped for a while, in a sheltered place... down a lane, outside a battered metal gate. Shabby blue with a thick piece of rope at the top. My father leapt out and stretched his long, lean body beside it, puffing on a cigarette. He glanced at the creatures in front of him, through the curls of smoke. Wide-eyed cows with a strong scent of manure gazed over the fence at us, tail-flicking the flies.

"Well, we've got an audience Wendy," he laughed, staring into their brown liquid eyes, "but at least they won't make any comment."

We opened up the square tin box displaying a picture of the Queen's coronation. We sat close together in the dip between the cream leather seats. Dainty soft cheese spread sandwiches, with straggly bits of red tomato escaping lay on crinkled greaseproof paper. Tiny fairy cakes with hundreds and thousands were pressed into the corners.

"Now, remember your manners. Imagine you're still sitting at the table," he reminded me, as I stuffed as many as possible into my mouth.

"But I'm really hungry Daddy."

"Me too. I don't think your mother gave our empty stomach enough consideration." He held the empty tin upside down and scattered the crumbs. We both giggled.

The warm, milky tea from the thermos flask was poured out evenly, with some reserved for later. My lean fingers enjoyed the heat of the grey plastic cup, as we sipped the sweet liquid.

"So... are you looking for fool's gold? Our class learnt about gold diggers in school last week. People trying to get rich by travelling to the other side of the world. Is that what we're doing?"

"Aah... well, maybe there's some truth in that, but we don't need to go quite as far. You can't go through life without a dream. If you see one door closing then shove another one open."

Our ancient Ford Prefect glided over the ridges, leaving deep tyre prints on the lane. I sat there clutching the seat, rocking from side to side, as we bounced over the bumps and slid into the dips. Meandered down narrow lanes, past faded country signposts and scurrying people.

"Might be hard work today, Wendy," he said after a while.

"Why's that?"

"I've got a lot of peat to dig up, many sacks to fill, so you can sit and watch from the car. No more long faces. Have you brought your latest Famous Five story?"

"Yes... but Daddy... I want to..."

"Now you must do as I say, you don't want to end up as one of those bog bodies."

I shuddered at the thought of what lay deep under the mud layers.

In front of us, there appeared a sweeping area of bleakness, a wide expanse of vibrant blue summer sky. Still and quiet yet eerie. Simple clusters of pink heather grew on the mounds and tufts. The late morning August heat, beating down on the dry earth. A plaintive sound of a young curlew passing over. Pools of thick mud interspersed between chunks of hardy green grass, for as far as you could see.

"You have to know what you're doing... where to go... the best place to dig."

"Yes."

He opened the window for a better view. The hot and blistering air outside, thin with no breath.

"Now… stay put…" The implements and sacks were dragged one by one out of the boot with hands encased in thick black gloves. A cotton cap pulled over thinning hair. "You're a bit exposed out here. The sun is beating down. I'll need this. You watch me from the car."

"Don't go too far away now, will you Daddy?" The tall, thin man with the curved shoulders and narrow hips sauntered off, preoccupied with the task ahead, and the distinct possibility of success. And… my words… faded… below the haunting calls of a wavering curlew and the bleak terrain.

~

The mud was swirling over the red sandals, and my thin pale ankles. Deep sludge clambered up both legs.

"Daddy, Daddy. Quick! Help! I'm sinking!" I screamed, as the squelching mire grabbed my flesh and sucked me down towards the earth. All I could think about were the layers of bodies underneath.

He turned and saw me, shrieked and leapt over the mounds, treading on the right places. His body, a fast moving blur of creams and browns. A stark white complexion. Thick tufts of bog slithered off heavy boots. A glowing cigarette stub bobbing up and down in the corner of his mouth.

"Hurry up Daddy… Daddy!"

"Wendy! I told you to stay in the car," he squealed, like the sounds of the mottled brown birds sailing overhead. Arms, sharp helicopter blades spinning ever closer to me. Tears slipped down my flushed cheeks and toes floated in the smelly liquid.

"Here! Quick! Grab this hand." Worn leather boots burrowed and dug into a firm place. "Now!" My father sprang forward, acquiring the strength from somewhere. He tugged and heaved, until I bounced out of the mud, folding myself around his splattered shirt. He stood there, clinging to me, with the breath taken out of him, unable to move or put words together. "It will be fine I promise. Hold me tight." My fingers made deep ridges in the back of his neck, as I inhaled the stale cigarette breath and fear.

"I'm sorry Daddy. I'm sorry," I sobbed. "I was only picking a bunch of those pink flowers for Mummy. I thought I could… that's all."

"It's OK… it's OK. Sssh."

He stroked my blond hair, gently pushing back the damp curls sticking to the side of the face.

"Now don't worry, you'll be fine. I shouldn't have..."

We gazed down at the dripping mud on both feet. I sat scrunched up on the front seat. A clammy smell made me dizzy.

"You'll stop shaking in a minute... a bit of a shock that's all. Oh dear... where's your sandal?"

"It's disappeared... will Mummy be cross?"

"Never mind, we'll think of a good story on the way home. Make one up. Now don't cry. The imagination is a wonderful thing, and I've never been short of it."

The dark mud was scraped off with an old bath towel. He moved rapidly between each toe, the left leg and then the right. Downward strokes leaving the skin red and stinging underneath. A travel rug appeared from the back seat and wrapped tightly around me. There I crouched, tucked underneath like a crumpled up parcel with only a piece of string and label missing. The remainder of the sweet, warm liquid eliminated some of the chill, as I settled back, eyes closing.

The green and cream Ford Prefect reversed out slowly. This time, I was unaware of the small towns and villages whizzing past, as the flickering colours bounced behind my eyelids. The only concern was for the missing sandal trapped in the bottom layers of the swirling bog.

We were both subdued and quiet. Father and daughter. The smell of peat lingering inside the car, the soft purr of the engine in our ears. I longed to be at home, playing in the child-filled street outside our semi, number 27. Bouncing a ball with Billy, or whizzing down the street with Mary, on an ancient blue bike. Knowing exactly the right time to squeeze the brakes, so you didn't somersault over the handlebars, as I had done last summer. My father's cigarette dangled on the end of his lip, as he puffed curly swirls of smoke around us. I felt nauseous but never spoke. The jagged moon was bright, and gleaming through the pink magnolia tree, as we pulled into the drive skidding on the tarmac. The chalky remnants of the last game of hopscotch were still on the pavement.

My mother was peeping out, eyes sparkling, a day on her own free from obligations. She waved. I waved back. Her hair was different, elegant, twisted round and piled up high with a fancy clip, like an intricate bird's nest in a sheltered tree. She lingered by the window looking delightful in green.

"Ssh... now I'll mention the red sandal... remember?"

"Yes Daddy," I said, hobbling out on one foot, dragging the tartan rug behind me.

"What happened to you two?" She gazed at me from top to bottom. "And what's she …?"

"It's a bit of a story love. Let's get inside first. I'd rather tell it sitting down."

"But, where's her…? Wendy? What's happened to the child? She's splattered with mud! What on earth…?"

"Mummy… I picked you… a bunch of pink flowers from the bog… but I dropped them… and they scattered… and I couldn't… and then…"

"Well. Never mind. That was very kind, so thoughtful." She kissed the top of my head, and squeezed a hand under the red tartan. "But, you won't be going back there again," my mother whispered, scrutinising my expression, "I don't know what came over me."

"No Mummy."

"In future he can have his own adventures. We'll stay on dry land."

The next morning, they were spread-eagled on the floor, surrounded by scraps of string, paper, a sack of peat and a sharp cutter.

"Can I help?" I watched with fascination as they chopped and folded, stacked up and counted little piles in front of me. My father's wide eyes glittered with possibility, my mother's dancing with amusement.

"No, you sit over there and watch."

"We're going to make firelighters out of the peat," my mother disclosed. "Your daddy is going to sell them in O'Flanagan's shop. On the front counter, near the till, so people will notice. Mrs O'Flanagan thinks people are certain to pick up a packet, with their morning shopping. Now, don't forget, under each tenth wrapper you're putting a pound note. That's what you wrote on the sticker. What we both decided. Remember? Are you listening?"

"Aaah… Of course I will. As if I'd forget something as important as that," he whispered, scanning my face. "It would be a terrible thing if I didn't… eh Wendy?"

But I stayed silent, swinging my bare feet under the chair, as he slipped one underneath the wrapper. He tied the string carefully in knots and put his thumb up in the air. All I could think of was, who would be the lucky recipient of my father's latest scheme?

9

Seeking Adventure

An essential ingredient of a 1950s and 1960s childhood was being able to roam wild and free, to taste the scent of danger on your lips, adrenalin racing through your body. Not a gadget in sight. How lucky we were. Parents thought nothing of their offspring disappearing for hours on end. Questions were never asked and answers rarely given. My friends, or cousins and I, were making future memories to tell our own children one day. Exploration of fields and hedgerows was part of enjoying a rich country childhood. Sometimes, we climbed on decaying farm machinery and created fascinating objects from bits and pieces lying around. Other times, we chased each other through the yard, past startled chickens and curious adults.

The summer holidays in Ulster lasted forever. This wasn't just through the eyes of us children, they actually did. Schools finished on the 28th June and we returned in the second week of September. The word 'bliss' is often overrated, but it's exactly the right word to describe such a joyful time. We cast our books aside, the chewed pencils and shabby school bags... and were released like brightly coloured balloons into the morning sky. The jagged patchwork fields and farmyards of County Down were our vast piece of heaven. Made for kids with a lot of energy and a highly developed sense of mischief. So naturally our pastimes and pursuits were varied and occasionally dangerous.

I lived a quiet, academic existence in term time, but when it was time to stay with my granny, life was magical. My cousins were bronzed, wiry little boys who had the letters spelling ADVENTURE emblazoned on their forehead. They came from a large family with few restraints. I was one of two, so life was very different.

The game we played two or three times every summer, was to see who could dash through the field of grazing cows, without upsetting the bull in the middle. My eldest cousin could have won a medal for sprinting. He was the cheekiest and made us all laugh. He was my hero! The rest of us watched with awe and a hint of envy, as he negotiated his way, zigzagging in and out of the loitering cows. Our grandad's prize bull watched him with some bemusement... but never seemed to move. The next one in age followed, not quite as fast as his brother, but still able to complete the task without causing a stir. The twins were next. They decided to dart through the cows together, leaping and hollowing, causing me to giggle nervously. The one slightly in front had the courage to pause and shout, "Get a move on. Come on."

The ancient gnarled bull, with the huge metal ring through his nose, shifted his hefty feet and turned slightly. The sharp blades of grass seemed more enticing.

Of course I was last as usual.

"Wendy's just a girl!" someone shouted.

"I'll show them," I thought, as I wiped my clammy hands on the red shorts and blackcurrant stained t-shirt. I was a skinny wee thing, sandals clinging to the end of very large feet. Maybe this was the moment to show my dwindling courage.

"Go on Wendy. You're the last. See if you can make it? Go on! Go on!"

I wanted to chicken out... wander off unnoticed, but this was the name of the game... and I was part of it.

The late August sun was beating down. I felt the heat stinging the top of my head and burning my pale arms. Off I went... the sweat was rolling down the back. I bounced over the grass avoiding the squelching cowpats. My soles squashed the clumps of clover, squeaking with the impact.

"Run Wendy... run!"

"He's coming after you!"

"Keep running!"

"What! Coming after me. No!"

I smelt the taste of fear and yesterday's Irish stew in my mouth. The pounding beast was getting closer. I daren't look round. Not now.

"Don't stop. He'll eat you alive. He's right behind you."

The boys were screeching and bouncing up and down. My ears hurt. Blond plaits were beating the back of my shoulders. Splash... I fell...

head first... into the stagnant ditch near the blackberry hedges. The skin of my grubby knees peeled off like a juicy tangerine. Slithers of blood rolled down the skin, as the jagged stones left their scratches.

The old brute of a bull peered over bellowing. You could see the disappointment in his eyes. He was foaming at the mouth and making shuddering noises near the edge. There I lay, with smelly water drenching my shorts and t-shirt. I tried not to cry... to call out. Tears trickled down my ruddy cheeks as a dry tongue licked the salty liquid.

"Are you alright?"

"He nearly snared you Wendy." Alan's words tumbled into the air.

I think I said yes, but I can't remember. By now I was whimpering... then I started to sob. The bull lifted his head, snorted, turned and wandered off. We watched him amble slowly towards a group of tail-flicking cows. It seemed to take for ages. My cousins waited for a moment, before taking turns to haul me out of the stagnant ditch. The whiff of wild peachy honeysuckle on an overhanging branch made me feel nauseous.

"Must have been your red shorts Wendy. Bulls don't like red." Alan, the oldest boy was keen to tell me, as my limp body untangled itself from the debris in the stream. The mud slithered down my legs, forming sticky blobs near the bottom.

"Let's not play that game again," said one of the twins. "What shall we tell our granny? She'll be cross, won't she?"

There was a pause... a moment of reflection. We crept around the safe side of the field, looking for the gap in the blackberry hedges. A whirring tractor could be heard in the distance. It was a ten minute stroll to granny's cottage. I limped and shivered all the way back, past fields of clover and birds nesting in spiky brambles. This was hopefully enough time for one of us to think of a convincing story...

~

When I was eight we moved to a small market town, where we played in the street and down by the old cattle market. There were more opportunities in the country to live the life that children dreamed of, but we brought our energy and imagination to the urban environment. Most of us were quite happy with our second-hand bikes, but how we envied the kids who owned the bright, shiny new models. Occasionally, we opened our mouths with admiration, when one of the richer boys or girls turned up on the latest Raleigh bikes, ringing their snazzy new bells.

One particular morning someone decided we should have a bike race. Not the usual bike race, but the fastest one ever. My friend Heather even suggested that it might be the fastest race in the world. Some of us wondered if this was a good idea, but no-one had the courage to speak up, or to be the 'afternoon's spoilsport'. Dave, the bossiest bike rider was feeling extra courageous today. His parents had gone out for the afternoon, so he seemed to have a hold over us. His sister pulled her tongue out at him and he mimicked her response. The seven of us lingered, waiting for further instructions. Most of the cars in the road were parked on the tarmac drives. The adults enjoying time away from their offspring, tending mature flowerbeds or enjoying a smoke, lounging on wooden stripy deckchairs.

Nothing could hinder the child prepared to hurtle down the street on the spinning silvery / black wheels, with sweaty hands clutching the plastic handlebars. The boys stood up, wobbling on their bikes. Each one of them expecting to win, as they waited with their killer expressions. The three of us girls lingered behind, wondering why we had agreed to take part. Hopscotch and hula hooping seemed to be a more attractive option.

"I'll go first," said Dave, puffing up his chest, determined to show the innate power of his new racer.

"We always go last" Mary and I complained.

He cast us a glance, as if we'd pinched his sherbet fountain and devoured the contents.

"Huh... you girls. This is how it's done."

Dave was off... all we could see was a flash of red and silver, the whirring of gigantic wheels and pedals, as the skinny lad in a scruffy pair of shorts disappeared... bouncing over the mounds... on his journey to the end of the street.

"He's a right show off that Dave O'Farrell," someone said loudly, with the leader of the pack being out of earshot. "Always thinks he's Desperate Dan."

"Break, break... now!" Billy shouted, jumping up and down.

The bike skidded to a halt... just in time... screeching... on the hot tarmac.

Everyone cheered, until they realised they might be next. Mary linked her arm in mine and squeezed it. I longed for my mum to wave her arms by our front gate and shout...

"Come in here now. I need your help Wendy."

But no-one ever says this when you want them to. I wouldn't have minded what she wanted help with and there would have been no request for extra pocket money. Mary and I drew lots to see who would go last. It turned out to be me. All the bikes were strewn on the ground. Their owners hot and glowing with ruddy cheeks and a sense of achievement.

"Come on Wendy. Your old bike can do it."

"Pedal as fast as you can." Dave couldn't help being sarcastic. "Build up a bit of speed."

"Speed... on that thing," someone giggled.

My spindly legs circled round as fast as was possible. Soon, I couldn't feel the feet on the pedals. The handlebars slipped under my fingers. The houses on the left including my own, number 27, flashed past with their gravel driveways and fragrant rose beds plonked in the middle.

"Brake... brake... Wendy... NOW."

Too late. Far too late. Over I tumbled... head spinning... over the barbed wire at the end of the street... into the cattle market. My flesh ripped open on the right ankle, spurts of blood scattering over the cotton ankle socks. The dark crows pecking on the ground below the factory wall scattered. Mary said afterwards my screams could have been heard on the other side of the Armagh Road. The other children raced down the street, leaving their entangled machines at the top.

"Are you okay?" shouted Heather. Her face was white.

"You didn't break when I told you!" Dave had all the answers as usual.

There was an opening of back doors, a squeaking of gates, the pounding of adult feet on the ground. My anxious group of friends moved to one side, as a worried mother in floral cotton leant over, brown hair swept up with a thousand hairclips.

"Mummy. I'm bleeding. It hurts."

"What's happened? Look at your leg... look at your bike."

"Och, you poor wee thing," said Mrs Mulligan kindly. "Whatever will you children do next?"

She scooped her four boys up in the folds of a voluminous dress. Dave O'Farrell looked sheepish as he sauntered slowly back up the street. He turned his head occasionally to witness me receiving first aid.

My father did his best to resurrect the old blue bike... but was never successful. It lay against the back wall for ages.

"I expect we'll have to save up for another one" he complained.

I didn't answer, as the decision had been taken never to get on a bike again. Not a sparkling brand new one or anyone else's second hand model. I would stick to the joys of hopscotch and hula hooping, both of which I excelled in. No one would ever persuade me otherwise... my mind was made up. The scar is still evident to this day on my right ankle. A painful reminder of one reckless Saturday in June.

~

Adventures don't always involve a shabby bike with dubious brakes, or a bull with fire in its eyes and anger in its belly. One day, my classmates and I were presented with one of the most adventurous moments of our teenage years. We could hardly wait.

"Make sure you don't lose the brown envelope," my mother reminded me, as I slid the rattling coins down into the depths of my leather school bag.

"It's a lot of money for what it is," my dad sniffed, before driving off in the Ford Prefect.

The coach was leaving for Armagh at 10.00 am, so being late for school was not on the agenda today. I scurried along over the bridge, breathing in the fumes of the passing cars with anticipation gathering in my body. Young children gathered in the playground of my old primary school with their hoops and balls, reminding me of my younger days there as a pupil. My mother's dusty old fashioned solicitor's office stood on the right, as I gathered up speed. Finding a good seat on the coach was everyone's ultimate aim, so eventually my fast walk turned into a sprint.

"Now boys and girls. Single file please. No running, shoving or pushing. We must arrive in one piece for Patrick Moore."

"Why's that Miss?" There was always one person who dared to be cheeky. It was the same boy who once enquired about the Holy Ghost in the school assembly hall.

Armagh Planetarium was a magnificent building. None of us knew what to expect, as we tumbled one by one off the step with flushed cheeks and animated conversation.

"Wonder what he's like?" asked one of the lads.

"He's a genius," someone answered. "My dad says he knows his stuff."

The person we were curious about was Patrick Moore (in those days he hadn't been knighted). He was in charge of the Planetarium and was known to be a bit eccentric. My heart skipped all over the place, as the teacher led us into the dome shaped room. Patrick Moore leapt out in front of us with a beaming smile. He was delighted to see all the children and gave a very passionate speech. I remember his kind face and the enthusiastic manner he displayed, while speaking about the magic of the stars and the universe. The talk was exhausting because there were a lot of facts to assimilate. He never seemed to pause for breath. We were in total awe of his magnetic personality.

"Now, are you strapped in boys and girls? We don't want you tumbling into space do we? We're switching the lights off now. Hold on."

I felt very nervous as we were plunged into darkness, with our seats rotating backwards. I let out a gasp. So did the others. One of the scariest moments I had ever experienced. We felt we were spinning amongst the stars. My hands clung to the armrests and I was almost afraid to breathe or move. We tried to listen to Patrick talking about the different constellations, as the stars twinkled above our heads. At times, it was difficult to keep up with his wild enthusiasm and passion, but we did our best.

~

Sometimes, when I stand in our Devon garden and gaze up at the unpolluted night sky, I am reminded of that special moment before I left Ulster. Sir Patrick Moore is no longer with us, but my fascination for the stars and the universe has never disappeared.

10

Grease Paint and a Feather Boa

It was Billy's fault. Always Billy's fault…

From the moment the nine pounder arrived in the front garden one July, in a navy carriage pram, he had been trouble. Big trouble! His sister Mary was my best friend and we shared the same dream. Fame! We both longed to be actresses, so we practised on the waste ground near our houses, with a feather boa and two wobbly pairs of grown-up heels. A spellbound audience in situ, if we could entice them with digestive biscuits and watery glasses of orange squash.

Mary spent her life avoiding her brother. So did I. He was hell-bent on shattering our plans. When his grandparents needed help on the farm, we were *ecstatic*. A Billy free day! Mary and I would join hands and do a funny kind of dance in our dressing up clothes, outside our house, number 27, under the pale pink magnolia tree. The adults nearby gave us a bemused smile, as they scuttled towards the shops at the top of the road. When we saw Mr McVeigh's blue Ford Zephyr leaving the drive, with Billy pulling faces from the back window, we were in *heaven* until his return.

"You're lucky Wendy. Your brother's very easy-going. He lies on the sofa munching chocolate, pretending he's playing for Manchester United. Mine follows me around, hell-bent on destruction."

I caught my mother in the kitchen at a difficult moment. She had her right arm down the sink and was pulling those strange faces, usually reserved for the birth of a lamb or a piglet on Granny's farm.

"Mummy?"

"Yeah?"

"Billy's a real pain. He's always messing up our plays. Won't take the parts I give him. He scatters the props and spreads them everywhere! *I could kill him!"*

"Well don't," she said, dangling a strange object in her hand. "Why not have a word with Mrs McVeigh? I'm sure she will be very sympathetic."

Later on that afternoon, I marched up the road past last night's game of hopscotch on the pavement and a shabby bike propped up against a fence. A rich smell of Irish stew laced with Guinness floated out of open windows. The heavy gate of number 15 was thrown open, and a sweet whiff of tea-roses filled my nostrils. I breathed in the scent and rang the bell. Mrs McVeigh was coated with flour. It clung to the ends of her fingers, with huge blobs splattered on her face. She was making a batch of cakes. Her husband's favourite. They were not quite as successful as usual...

"Yes?" she said. There was something about the tone that made me hesitate.

"I've... er... come... about your Billy."

"What about him?"

Mary waved out of her bedroom window, thumbs up, admiring my audacity.

"He spoils all our plays. Doesn't do as he's told. *Ever!* Won't listen to me... ruins all of our ideas! *He gets on my nerves.*"

"Well... what does a ten year old girl like you know about nerves... eh?"

The flour leapt into the air and over her feet. Green eyes focused on mine.

"Oh... I thought... you..."

"Now go away and don't bother me anymore. Skedaddle."

The door closed and Mary pulled a face from up above.

"Damn. I guess we're stuck with him forever," she called down.

I slunk back, hands in my pockets... slowly at first... blond pigtails bobbing over the shoulders. Soon, my pace quickened... the red sandals bounced on the pavement. I flew into the house, up into the tiny bedroom. A plan emerged. It was foolproof. Better not share it with the adults just yet. My birthday spell book would hold the answer. Page 62 looked the most interesting. Only three ingredients needed. Mary might be down in a minute. She would be a great help. No one was ever going to scupper our thespian dreams.

Saturday arrived very quickly, the one we had been waiting for. Sadly,

Billy had not been eliminated, despite several late evenings with the book under torchlight. His sister and I were convinced that he had been spoken to, so maybe it had been worth leaping up their garden path.

Outside my bedroom window, the pale pink magnolia petals were obliterating the drive. One or two hovered on the side of a branch waiting to follow. Without slipping over, my scuffed red sandals made their way downstairs and through the open door of the garage. There were only a few children gathered in the street today, huddled on the pavement playing hopscotch, or riding bikes as fast as they dared, past open windows and black metal gates. The occasional bouncing ball and the gentle swish of skipping ropes, in the background. Soon, when given the signal, the children would be off, with one eye on the clock and the other on the adults who had just given them permission. There would be a jumping off chairs and a sliding under Formica tables. A chance to disappear down the street to number 27, with laughter and anticipation. Ours, was the right hand house of a pair of semis, with a Ford Prefect parked badly outside. On the other side of fluttering net curtains, there was a loud buzz from the tiny black and white TV set. This was 1963, when the little cream and brown oblong box ruled supreme in everyone's front sitting rooms. The moment when conversation changed forever. The chance to watch your hero kicking a ball around a pitch, if you were football fans like my dad and brother, rather than sitting huddled around the radio.

At the back of the garage were several cardboard boxes and an old trunk. My hands lifted up the flaps, while I peeped at the inner contents and drew breath. The magic of endless possibilities and different characters lay inside.

"I've got the check-list." My brother rushed out of the door, shaking a piece of paper and a chubby pencil. "But I want to watch the football. I don't want to…"

Today on the 25th May 1963 was the cup final. Manchester United were playing Leicester City and Michael couldn't wait to see his hero Bobby Charlton. He had been reluctantly enticed outside, with the promise of my tube of lovehearts. Standing beside me, he awaited further instructions, in a new pair of football boots bought especially for the occasion.

"It's not starting yet! You can watch the football when you've helped me. Bobby Charlton can wait."

The sweets were dangled in front of him. He grabbed them quickly before I could change my mind. For the next ten minutes, we sat cross-legged and sorted out the main props and costumes in the boxes.

"Can't you do the rest yourself?" he said eventually, shoving the lovehearts in his mouth, two at a time.

"You're supposed to read the messages before you chew them," I grumbled.

"I just like the taste. Not bothered with all those soppy messages. Ugh!"

"It'll only take another few minutes," I promised, as we dived into piles of cotton shirts, old curtains, woollen jumpers, glittering dresses and my cream feather boa.

Before I could say Matt Busby backwards, Michael had escaped and rushed back through the kitchen door. I imagined him and my dad slouching on the sofa preparing for the cup final. My dad would have the usual cigarette balancing cleverly on the bottom of his lip. Soon, the smoke would be gathering around and above them in huge swirls. I wasn't bothered about the result of the match, but they were. More important to me, was the sheer joy and escapism that my latest production would provide. When I wasn't scribbling my latest story, I dreamed of being an actress. Sport was very low on the agenda.

Soon, all those children as disinterested in football as me, would arrive in our garage, anxious to see what part they would play and which costume had been selected for them. There was a clatter of many feet and there they were: Heather, Joan, Jenny, Mary and... Billy, looking slightly sheepish. I handed over a pile of old clothes, before they had time to complain about my choices. Grubby hands grabbed them by the collars, sleeves and dangling zips. Bodies slid into long skirts and dresses and wriggled into stripy trousers. Skinny legs arrived in clumpy shoes, or wobbled in high stilettos. Feet were dragged noisily over the garage floor. Billy, who had been very well behaved for ten minutes, couldn't believe his luck. His favourite thing in the whole world was still there. He snatched the moulting feather boa and shuffled out onto the tarmac drive, trying not to skid on the pale pink magnolia petals. Joan looked on jealously, deciding that contentment would have to be found by settling for a magician's shabby black cloak. We all ignored her attempts to scare us when she found a magic wand in the bottom of the wooden trunk.

A giggling Heather kept falling over in the baggy trousers with the brightly coloured braces. It was so easy to imagine that she was a clown, in the centre of the ring bowing to the audience. Mary, my best friend, in a diamond tiara, swirled and twirled in a vivid blue taffeta ball gown. She was no longer the eleven year old girl from number 7, but a famous actress enjoying the admiring audience.

"And what will you wear Wendy?"

They were all intrigued to see my choice, as I lifted my granny's shimmering Cossack hat out of the bottom. On a past visit to Russia, my grandad had bought her a new one. I was so pleased he did this, as I couldn't imagine her feeding the chickens without it plonked on her grey curls.

"What's that thing?" asked Heather. "It looks like an animal."

I placed it on my head to show her.

Everyone giggled. Joan touched the quivering fur, her hand peeping out from under the cloak. The others jumped up and did the same.

"My grandad brought it back from Russia for my granny," I announced proudly. "She looks like a princess in it."

"Where's that? Never heard of Russia," Billy shouted loudly.

"It's the other side of the world silly. Miles away. Takes forever to get there and come back. You've got to go on lots of boats."

"Why does he go there?" Mary was intrigued. The others were fascinated.

"Cos he likes the Russian people."

"Are they different from us?"

"Dunno."

"I thought he was a dairy farmer in County Down."

"Course he is, stupid... you can be both."

"My mummy says, the best place in the world to go on holiday is Newcastle in County Down or Kilkeel," Joan told us.

"Or Donagadee," added Billy, "in a caravan."

"My daddy says we'll never go anywhere else but Ireland."

"Well, he goes to Russia and it's a great place," I sniffed, lowering the Cossack hat onto my head at the right angle, so I didn't disappear completely.

"So where's Michael?" asked Billy, plucking feathers from the boa.

"Watching the match as usual. It's the Cup Final, but... he did help me sort everything out before the play. You're the only boy I know who doesn't like football."

"We'll miss him being the Lone Ranger. Running around and digging us in the ribs. Having to lie still for five minutes, because he's shot us in the back."

I slid slowly into a long black skirt and matching jacket.

"Now I look like one of those Russian ladies," I told them, swishing the folds from side to side. "Doesn't go with my red scuffed sandals though. I wanted my mummy's black stilettos, but she's not ready to give them to the dressing-up box yet."

"My mummy wears stilettos too, but they give her big lumps on the side of her toes," said Mary.

"They're called bunions." Heather was adamant. "All ladies have them. *My* mummy's got two."

"It's because you don't wear sensible shoes."

We all stared at Billy, who was flicking feathers with his right hand.

"Shut up Billy!" someone shouted.

"Well... that's what my Dad says."

When the topic of footwear had faded, everyone was handed a neatly typed sheet with our play set into scenes. The typewriter received for my tenth birthday had brought me so much joy. As a budding writer or actress, depending on the day of the week, owning one was all I had ever wanted. My fingers sped across the keys and my creativity exploded onto the pages, as different characters were created.

"There aren't so many of us today," I said. "Some people are on holiday, but you've all got something to say. Now, Billy... no changing characters... wandering off... digging people in the ribs or swearing."

"Okay! Okay! Keep your hair on."

Everyone cheered, wondering if he would keep his promise.

My mother appeared in front of us, pleased to escape from the noisy football match indoors. I heard the cheering from the sitting room as she came through the back door. A tray of yellow striped glasses with lemonade in and pieces of buttered ginger cake were pounced on immediately.

"It's half time, I thought I'd come out for some fresh air. Your daddy's really pleased. Manchester United are winning 1-0. A great goal from Denis Law! Your brother's very happy."

"Oh," I said, trying to sound interested.

"Well... I wouldn't have recognised any of you." Her admiring glances went from one to the other. "What time does your play start Wendy?"

"Twenty minutes."

"Well, I'll come down and watch it when I've cleared up. It's too lovely to be stuck indoors." She looked up at the sun glinting through the magnolia. "Hmn… just smell that blossom. It's so hot the birds are hiding in the trees."

"Ok Mummy."

"Of course," she said, with a whisper, "it's a pity you had to give all that money back last time. Your father wasn't very happy when you knocked on the doors and charged people to watch the play."

"No," I blushed, as my friends sniggered at my misdemeanour. "I won't do it again. Promise."

"Well… I expect you got a bit overexcited… there's worse things I suppose."

"*Yes.*" I quickly gathered up the others behind me, before anyone could comment. We traipsed off, clutching our baggy trousers and ball gowns, through the black metal gate, past the other semis, into our play area behind the cattle market.

Once there, our group prepared to set up the few props we had carried down with us, while we waited for the non-paying audience to arrive. Soon, yet another performance, with a mixture of laughter and a sprinkling of gravity would unfold. There would be the usual problem of feet pointing in the wrong direction and children skidding and falling over. Maybe the odd argument and an occasional tear when someone wouldn't listen. Below the tall concrete walls of the cattle market, with the circling black crows perched above, we bounced and leapt from one scene to another. Although we had great fun during the plays, the best moments were always those at the finale, when we clutched each other's hands and took a bow in our greasepaint and sparkle.

Little did I know back then in the 1960s, that my grandfather's aunts, the Kirkpatricks, were stepping out in the theatre and dance halls in the early 1900s. This was long before my much loved career as a Head of Drama had ever been thought of. The moment I heard about these hidden ancestors, I understood why my love of storytelling and innate passion for the theatre has followed me throughout my life.

11

All Because of Mary

We perched in the front row, freshly scrubbed with pink cheeks, feet sliding over the newly polished parquet floor. Crushed and squashed together, unable to breathe with the buzz of anticipation. I sat in the middle, arms folded, bony knees peeping above the white socks.

"Do you think there's something happening?" whispered Barbara O'Malley in my left ear. "All the sixth formers at the back are giggling and talking."

I was about to turn round and give the question some consideration when the Headteacher, a delightful and charming man, flew onto the stage. His voluminous black cloak floated through the air. He quivered above the chairs like a shabby black crow and placed a finger on his lips.

"Sssh!" he said. "I have something to tell you so please listen. Now, those at the back might have an inkling, but you first formers will not."

We shook our heads, curious for the next part of the mystery to unfold.

"Now, I bet you have no idea who is hiding behind the curtains," he said, in the manner of someone who couldn't wait to share his secret. "I'll just tell you... we have a very special person... waiting to come and meet you."

"Excuse me sir, would it be the Holy Ghost?" said Bobby Johnson unable to miss an opportunity.

"It is not!"

"Well, then it's got to be Jesus Christ."

"And who says that, young man? I will talk to you later."

There was a collective snigger from the four rows at the back. A red-faced Bobby slid down into the seat scowling.

The maroon faded curtains began to twitch and quiver... and out the visitor popped.

"Here she is. Mary Peters. A previous Head Girl. She's just come second in the Commonwealth Games in the shot put event for Northern Ireland, and has kindly returned to tell us all about it."

In a navy blue track suit, with blond hair tied back and a beaming smile she dangled the glittering medal in front of our eyes. My heart thumped under the thin blue blouse as Mary gave the assembly an inspirational speech. The Headteacher hovered on her right, flushed and proud.

"Aim high boys and girls. Work hard in school and everything is achievable. That's what I did. So… follow your dreams."

We all cheered, and clapped our hands so much we thought the skin would split or explode.

"Do you think she'll come and see us in Domestic Science?" asked my occasional friend Jane, as we moved out of the hall in single file.

"I don't know."

"Cos you can't make decent cakes!"

"Neither can you."

"But mine always look better than yours."

"Who says…?"

Jane was not only right about the cakes but anything else domestic too. I didn't know how to switch on the cooker and my ingredients either ended up on the floor or swirling around at the bottom of my satchel. But I don't mind telling all of you… I was a dab hand at rolling pastry.

Mary Peters was due to arrive in our lesson at any time. Could this be the moment I had been waiting for? There was to be a competition for the longest piece of pastry in the class. The girls stood there, rolling pins poised, sleeves rolled up, ready to dive into the huge mixing bowls with the spatulas and wooden spoons. Mary's smile peeped through the window. She waved and crept in to the sound of applause, the sparkling silver medal around her neck.

"Ready… steady girls… go!" Miss McKeown blew the whistle and we were off! Oblivious to anyone else. Before long my fat, misshapen lump had turned into the longest piece of pastry ever seen. Perhaps it was a miracle! It crawled over the sides of the table, becoming strangely discoloured as the size of it grew and grew. Mary Peters looked on with a mixture of amusement and awe, chuckling at our floury cheeks and chins, and the rolling pins flying over the pastry.

The whistle blew again and we all stood back to get Mary's blessing. She wandered around the tables, stopping to admire the different shapes, prodding with her fingers and poking about.

"Wendy's pastry is touching the floor Miss and it's really dirty," the girl nearest me complained.

"I don't care about the colour Maggie, it's the quality that counts. You just worry about your own."

The teacher beckoned our special visitor to the front of the class and whispered in her ear. After a few minutes Mary ambled over to my table.

"I think you're the winner," she said, touching my pastry snake. With flushed cheeks she leant over and kissed me. "Wendy gets the sixpence... and all of you girls can hold the medal after her."

"Thank you Mary," I said, clasping the silver medal to my chest. "I'll pass it on to someone else in a minute."

At the end of the lesson Mary Peters opened the door and waved, disappearing down the long hot corridor on her way to another class.

"I was very impressed Wendy with your hidden talents this morning," said the Domestic Science teacher over my left shoulder. "So naturally I will be expecting great things from you now."

Miss McKeown's slim body encased in blue tweed, hovered in front of us. It was two weeks later, after all the excitement. Wire-rimmed glasses bounced up and down on a snub nose as she peered over them. Some of us, especially me, were still floating round on another planet, following the visit of our very own VIP.

"Are you listening girls?" she asked, checking our pencils were poised and an untouched page lay between our fingers. We formed a semi-circle around her, fascinated by the enthusiasm with which she threw herself down in front of the sink, legs sliding, shoes flying, neck elongated amongst the bottles of sink cleaners and cloths.

"Now..."

We were captivated by the jerky arm movements and the rise and fall of her soft Ulster voice.

"Look over here... *here*... this is a U bend."

"A what?"

To say I was disappointed would be an understatement. The suggestion in our last Domestic Science lesson that this might be an important part of our future life was unbelievable. Here was our young teacher, all scrunched up in a most undignified manner, under a bit of grey plastic.

"Are you all right in there Miss?" someone giggled, as the erratic movements developed into twisting and tugging various bits and pieces with her fingers.

"I'm fine… *now stand back.*"

"Stand back Miss? Why?"

A tiny amount of liquid, an elastic band and a few strange objects emerged in the palm of her yellow glove.

"Yuk!" someone said, pulling a funny face.

"Now come over here and check what I've done. It's very important for you girls to know what to do next."

Slithers of blue tweed caught the light as the teacher huffed and puffed and beckoned us forward.

"What's a U bend anyway?" asked Jane.

"It catches all the nasty bits… and the smells!"

We could just about hear Miss McKeown's voice, as a group of children from another class rushed down the corridor giggling and laughing.

"*I'm not going to have a U bend!* I won't have time. I'm going to be a doctor," said Karen.

"Well young lady everyone has a U bend and you'll have to clean it. It won't be your husband's job."

I wonder if I've got one, I thought, remembering the occasions when my mother skidded around our kitchen looking flushed, with a yellow bucket in her hand.

My classmates tried very hard not to chuckle, as Miss McKeown emerged bottom first, doing a nifty little routine as she shuffled towards us. Her brood scattered like crumbs of soda bread on a dirty breakfast plate. A dishevelled appearance and ruddy cheeks made us gasp. She regained composure in a remarkable space of time, her leather belt once again clinched in at the waist. We noticed a thick ladder escaping down the American tan stockings.

"Now girls… did you get a good peep? Does anyone want to take a closer look before I…?"

"Er… no thanks Miss," Heather muttered.

"Now, don't forget," she reminded us. "A U bend should be cleaned once a week. As you have seen, all sorts of nasty things accumulate down there."

We all feigned interest and someone's stomach rumbled loudly. "There are twenty minutes before lunch, so go away and draw the internal workings. Label everything clearly please."

In clusters, we drifted back to the Formica tables peering over towards the sink for a tiny bit of inspiration. All of us longed to be in the dinner queue instead, for a huge dollop of Irish stew followed by sweet pink custard. Miss McKeown took the opportunity to tidy herself up in the store cupboard. She gazed into the wall mirror pulling various bits up and down. Hair grips pinged on the floor beside her, as her rosy cheeks were dabbed with a fresh tissue.

Five attempts later I was so pleased to hear the bell. The strange shape in front of me on the page was unrecognisable. Without any further thought, I slid the exercise book between two others at the bottom of the pile and took a deep breath. Hopefully, the Domestic Science teacher would fall asleep or get distracted before my scruffy offering was pulled out of the pile. I might have been 'ace' at rolling pastry but understanding U bends was a different matter.

~

The grey skies above were weeping moisture into the chilly November air. A collection of fifth form girls rushed up the steps of the pavilion, scattering sweat and frizzy curls.

"Miss Irwin's in a bad mood today. Must be boyfriend trouble. Watch out! She's on the prowl," said one, banging her hockey stick on the green peeling paint, as she headed towards the lukewarm showers and the smell of carbolic.

Karen and I shuffled past the rest of the class, weary from a morning's cooking, as we crept under the dripping horse chestnut tree. Our legs slithered and slid on the mounds of mud they'd left behind. An elaborate spider's web floated in the mist near our fingers, as we peeped into the branches. Leather-encased toes kicked the earth, and the elastic under our blue sports socks squeezed the flesh. Familiar black crows were circling over the bleak school pitch. Raucous sounds filled our ears as they swooped from one tree to the other.

"Now girls. I want to see a bit of action. *No groaning please.* It's my job to make sportswomen of you all, like Mary Peters. If she can do it so can you. Don't just stand there! Wendy... no lingering on the side as usual... doing nothing. Keep your eye on the ball."

"Yes... Miss." My voice shivered, as the cold filtered into thin bones and a tiny frame. I longed to be in English or Art, not in PE with Miss Irwin in a navy blue sweaty tracksuit with a silver whistle dangling from her neck. Even drawing a U bend was preferable to this.

The game started. The girls threw their bodies after the ball, twisting and chasing its passage across the pitch. Screaming. Screeching. Calling from one to another. Near the side-line was a perfect place to hide. I thought about warm soda bread slices dripping with butter, a penny liquorice wheel spinning into a grateful mouth or giggling over a glass of dandelion and burdock with my granny. Blue eyes wandered up... up... into the still grey sky to the vapour of a passing plane and a swooping bird leaving its warm nest.

Miss Irwin's harsh voice echoed. "Move it girl. Run for the ball. 'Now!' I said. Don't just stand there, put your stick up. We're playing Belfast Academy next week. I'll make champions of you yet."

Tiny feet sprang over the soggy earth, spreading clods of soil and particles of grass. Perspiration trickled over my nose. I leapt up, higher than I had ever done before, fingers clutching the new hockey stick.

"*Ouch... Aaaaah...!*"

The hockey ball landed with a thud on my chin. I crumpled into a navy soggy mess near the edge. Several stars flashed above my eyes. There was a wave of nausea. A rumbling sound rushed towards my body, the pounding of many feet and numerous eyes peered down. I wondered what Mary Peters would have done next.

"She's fallen over Miss. I think she's skidded."

"Oh dear." Miss Irwin hovered over me. "I don't know, Wendy, you've spent half the term daydreaming... and when you listen to me for a change... this happens."

"Does it hurt a lot?" asked my friend Jane quietly.

"Yes, it really stings. I think I've cracked it. It feels all..."

"You'll have a big bruise there for weeks." The hockey teacher lifted me up gently and stroked my brow.

"And a dirty chin," someone giggled.

"Well... these things happen... Come on... Let's get you in the warm. Now *youse girls* can stop gawking!"

"Will she be able to do PE next week Miss?" someone enquired, as I ambled back to the pavilion, arm in arm with the teacher. Rows of neat, semi-detached houses peeped over the playing field hedges, their bevelled windows dazzling with neon.

"No, I think she'll need a week off. Such a pity. Just when she was getting the hang of it. Wendy will just have to sit and read her books. No climbing ropes or leaping over a box for her. No gold medals eh...!"

Our new hockey teacher led me back across the pitch, the silver whistle swinging from side to side. I tried very hard to hide my smile. Maybe, sometimes... a bit of pain was worth it.

12

The Lost Sheep

"Can I borrow your vicar Jane... *please?*"

I leant forward and tugged the crumpled cotton blouse of the person beside me.

"What's wrong with your own?" someone in front whispered.

"She never goes to church... ever." Jenny could hardly wait to spit the words out. "It isn't natural."

The gathering of flushed cheeks and pigtails circled me, the young girl sitting quietly at the desk.

"You're the only one in our class who doesn't. Wendy's a heathen. That's what my mummy thinks," Anne whispered, opening her pristine leather bible at the right page.

"No... I'm not. My daddy says we're agnostic."

"Agnostic, what's that?"

"I don't know... he just says."

The thought of a new word with a mysterious meaning made them speechless. They tutted and huffed, sliding back into the uncomfortable seats ready to outshine one another. How I envied them rushing off to church twice on a Sunday in their best clothes and turning up on Mondays with all their stories. None of the girls ever complained about a full day of worship. It was their life and how I longed to do the same.

"*So can I borrow your vicar?* Write down some details. Anything. Please." My friend tore a piece of paper from the exercise book and slid it slowly across the desk.

Jane smiled over. "You'll be okay," she said quietly. "Never mind them."

The teacher was hovering near the front, arranging and rearranging the few items on her desk.

"Make sure your books are open now children. Our special visitor will be here in a minute."

"Yes Miss."

I looked down and scanned the words quickly.

"I think she's wearing her best suit today," Jenny whispered, as the RE teacher tottered around on red high heels, like a novice skater on thin ice. "And we know why that is."

It was nine thirty. The frayed poster of Jesus, the bookshelves and rows of neat prayer books below had been dusted to perfection.

The Reverend Small burst into the classroom with his shiny dog collar and moist forehead. On time. He had the gift of being able to focus on every pupil immediately, with razor-sharp, blue eyes. The morning light flickered on the cream blinds as he whizzed past.

"Miss Knox," he beamed.

"Reverend Small," she said, holding in the tightly belted figure and tossing auburn curls sideways.

"Morning boys and girls. How *nice* to see you again. Monday morning... the start of the week. A perfect time to tell me about your Sunday."

Squeaky black brogues skidded on the parquet floor as he danced around the classroom in search of his prey. "Who's going to start first? How about you, young lady?"

Every eye settled on the first victim. The room was silent. You could feel the collective breath and smell the heady scent of the teacher's rose perfume.

"What's your name?"

"Wendy."

"Please start my dear."

"I'd like to talk about the Reverend Quinn," I announced, leaping up, clutching the torn-out piece of paper.

The adopted vicar was spoken about with eloquence and passion. His outstanding qualities shone like a sneaky silver torch after midnight. There was nothing this man couldn't do or hadn't done.

A snigger curved around the classroom. Miss Knox clung to the desk like a fragile vessel about to capsize. The boys were cheering loudly. The vicar spun round on the tips of his brogues waving a bible.

"No need for applause children. I think there is however... some natural talent in our midst... in fact quite inspirational."

The edges of the name-scrawled desk rose up and plucked me back into the seat. For a moment I couldn't breathe, like a trapped fish searching for air.

"What do you think Miss Knox?"

"Yes, Reverend Small," she hissed, staring at me, the girl perched uncomfortably in the back row. "Very inspirational indeed."

"Now, where do you live young lady?"

"Portadown sir."

"Aah. How interesting. The Reverend Quinn lives ten miles away in Banbridge. This is not his parish. He's a good friend of mine."

There was a united gasp. A holding of breath. A few boys giggled. Jane covered her eyes and blushed. There would be a penance to pay for lending out her vicar.

"You seem to know more about him than I do. He'll be quite impressed with those hidden talents. So tell me… do you go to church or do you not?"

"No, Reverend Small, I don't."

"Oh dear."

Everyone chuckled except Jane, who whispered, "It's fine. Never mind, we're in this together."

My eyes stared out beyond the noisy classroom, to the muddy hockey pitch and the slanting roof of the green pavilion. I could almost touch the leaves of the horse chestnut tree stroking the window pane. The vicar's warm breath tapped me on the shoulder.

"Aah… a lost sheep Miss Knox. Such a pity. We must welcome the poor child back into the fold before it's too late."

~

It was the morning of the bath. The weekly session. A GRAND OCCASION. A chance to wash behind the ears and other mucky bits. Circling steam and muddy knees. Moisture-dripping green walls and a yellow duck… bottom up. There was never enough water to fill the tub. A slow… slow… trickle from the left hand tap. Soap disappearing behind the frayed flannel and a lumpy sponge beyond use. All this and I was expected to come out clean. Outside the metal frames of the open window, you could see the gentleness of the pink magnolia tree circling above the path. Delicate petals spiralled downwards on to the tarmac. My father's blue Ford Prefect with the soft leather seats was parked badly in the drive. As I searched for the carbolic floating in the murky depths, a sound could be heard. Clenched knuckles pushing the metal gate, a loud huffing and puffing, and a few choice words under the breath. It was him, a new visitor, spurred on by the thought of much needed salvation at number 27. I rose up and took a flying leap, like a giant whale scattering the sea, leant over the banister at the top of the stairs, water trickling down my spindly legs.

"Daddy, Daddy, it's the vicar. It's him… the Reverend Small."

"You get back in the bath. Your brother's got to get in there after you. Leave the man of the cloth to me."

I slunk back into the tiny bathroom and peeped out, with just enough cover to stay invisible in the folds of steam. Slippery elbows hovered above the basin.

The Reverend Small was skipping and hopping up the path now, in a freshly pressed suit, trying to avoid the grubby soap suds from an earlier bath. Another blocked drain… to be sorted out. Short cropped hair rose above the shiny dog collar and oval flushed cheeks. Stubby fingers clutched an old red bible. He was humming 'The Lord's My Shepherd', out of tune. It felt good to know God was on his side. Determined to meet possible defeat head on, the vicar carefully considered the final hurdle that would take him to the steep steps of number 27. He gulped outside the house, like a dark, moody fish hovering above the water.

"Can I help you?" My father was scowling, in a white singlet, unshaven, with a woodbine dangling from his lips. One foot perched in the door, in case the vicar invited himself in for lunch.

"Aah… Just the person I… Mr…"

"Yes?"

"I've come about your daughter."

"She's in the bath."

The Reverend Small looked up crossly, muttering, through the pink petals of the magnolia tree. I ducked behind the window sill and the curling steam.

"Och… not on a Sunday…?"

"There's no set time for having a bath Reverend Small. You can clean yourself any day of the week."

"I think you should be sending her to church before it's too late. The Almighty doesn't miss a thing. Watching over all of us. Even me…"

"Huh."

"Just because you don't believe!"

"No I won't."

"Have you got a good reason? Remember God is listening." His voice crackled.

"No... and I don't have to give one either."

"Well... she's a fallen sheep and we need to welcome her back into the fold before it's too late. Nearly twelve and the only one in her class who doesn't attend church."

"That isn't a problem. She's alright as she is. Now we don't want any more visits. Goodbye VICAR."

The bath water was shivery cold. The family sponge clearly disintegrating. Carbolic soap was floating in pieces on the grey suds. I slid back in slowly, listening to the sweet sounds of the church bells. Outside, the scuttling of the neighbours' feet on the pavement and the loud laughter from the four noisy boys next door could be heard. Dressed in Sunday best and clutching their prayer books tightly, the family were anxious to find the best seats in the house.

The quivering Reverend Small adjusted the dog collar sticking to his neck and wiped a warm brow with a clean hanky. After lunch he would pray for my lost soul and ask the Almighty for divine intervention.

My Irish childhood was very unusual. Our education involved religious segregation at both primary and secondary school, but my parents were English and didn't toe the line. In the front and back gardens and on the chalky pavements in our road, Catholics and Protestants played happily together and adults lived side by side and developed strong relationships. My mother and I often slipped into number 25 for a cup of tea and a bit of a natter. Mrs Mulligan was one of her best friends. Her religion was never mentioned, but they chatted and shared family stories, below the painting of the Pope smiling down kindly upon us. The new font in the hall was never mentioned, as we lingered by the doorway saying our goodbyes. Perhaps my mother never knew I was an 'Honorary Catholic'. On one other occasion, I remember our invitation to dinner with the lady who lived at number 29. A quiet, kind soul who devoured her dinner nightly underneath a framed photograph of Ian Paisley and family. She gave him a good spit and polish every week so the young politician always looked his best.

The only time the odd comment was made was on the 12th and 13th July. The thudding, repetitive sound of the Lambeg drums on the Protestant marches each year, filled your ears and made your head burst.

Men wearing orange sashes and smartly pressed black suits marched past, heads held high, with some younger members twirling batons. There was always a slight relief when the noise ended and routine returned to the local streets. Our Catholic neighbours soon settled back into their normal lives knowing that there would be no mention of King Billy for another year.

Once, when I was sitting in the assembly hall in the fourth year our Headteacher announced something he had never said before.

"Now everyone, this morning we are having a Catholic boy joining our school. When he comes in I don't want anyone to look round. Do you understand, children?"

Naturally there was a uniform swishing of heads, a sound not unlike pampas grass fluttering in the wind. This blond, handsome teenager stepped inside and all of the girls were smitten. Our natural instinct was to work out very quickly if he looked any different from the other boys. He didn't. Would he behave differently? He didn't. I still wonder years later how he felt arriving in a very Protestant environment.

A special moment had arrived at last. One I never felt would materialise. My first church visit. I was fifteen and wearing a new dress for the occasion. Our local vicar had been very good at calling me 'a lost sheep' so he would have been delighted at seeing my angelic appearance in shiny blue, a straw hat perched on top. The friendly Minister at the quaint country church hovered near the door to welcome his faithful congregation.

"This is my niece," my aunt said proudly as I clutched my three little cousins' hands. He strolled towards the pulpit, gazing at his flock dressed in their Sunday best. I imagined him looking up to God for guidance as the service went into full swing. The young girl perched in the middle of the congregation gave him the perfect inspiration he needed. Squashed between my aunt in cream and my ruddy cheeked uncle I sat there mesmerised, arms folded in anticipation. The leather bible clutched so firmly between my hands that I was afraid to let it go. Suddenly… there was a loud rumbling and grumbling. A gurgling sound echoed in the little stone church and bounced off the walls either side.

"Aah… someone's obviously thinking of their dinner," he chuckled leaning forward. My adolescent cheeks exploded like a red juicy apple plucked from an Armagh orchard . My aunt patted my hand and grinned.

"We're having rabbit stew," I said quietly. He nodded with approval as did the congregation before continuing with the rest of the service, the words of which I remember perfectly. I sang the hymns at the top of my voice and I listened to every word the Minister uttered. We recited the Lord's Prayer under our breath and shook his hand. I thought I'd arrived in heaven.

13

Food for Thought

The one smell that evokes the fond memories of Ulster is the wonderful aroma of soda bread and wheaten farls. I spent my childhood devouring as much of these as I could; fresh from the oven, split in half, and dripping with butter and hedgerow jam. The tangy taste of Irish potato bread, squeezed against a piece of bacon and an egg or two, from those blessed chickens, always made one's young life complete. So, imagine the shock when arriving in England in 1968, to find that life over here did not include these daily treats.

At the age of sixteen, I wandered around the local bakers, being met with wide-eyed curiosity and the shaking of heads. So in their absence, I knew, the next best thing would be to buy a griddle and make my own. Easier said than done. The local department store had not heard of this gadget and could not even understand my accent. Eventually, it dawned on me that my life would need to carry on without my favourite nibbles, and a liking for plastic sliced bread would have to be developed. My dear grandmother was most perturbed. She sent over mini parcels of soda bread and wheaten farls, wrapped up in the familiar greaseproof for her deprived granddaughter. Naturally, by the time they arrived with me they were often stale. Now of course, you can buy these in all the supermarkets but I'll never forget that childhood longing.

Perched on the step at Hillside Cottage with my grandmother, below the hot summer skies, I shelled garden peas into a galvanised bucket, trying to imagine how long it would take to fill it to the top. With little mathematical ability, poor knowledge of probability and only aged seven going on eight, I could never work out an answer. Neither could she! We weren't very good at counting but we had so much fun. Some of the summer holidays in County Down were spent topping and tailing gooseberries. My favourite… but I often ended up with a sore tummy. I still feel nostalgic today when I notice these on supermarket shelves. My mind drifts back to those balmy days, with my toes dangling in the dust, when storytelling and the imagination first developed. Granny told me many amusing stories about growing up with her sisters in Manchester, before she moved to Ireland. I, of course, listened avidly to these tales, as the sound of the firm gooseberries pinged into a pot. Later they would be turned into a delicious pie with dollops of cream or thick gooey custard. I would leap over excitable chickens and dive off the swing in the apple orchard, to get my grubby hands on a gooseberry.

Sometimes in the late summer, I took part in a wild competition with the birds, as we all attacked the hedgerows for the latest plump and glistening blackberries. Soon I realised that the idea of two for the mouth and one for the pot was a decent reward, as I scrambled for the juiciest sweet treasures. Before long my summer shorts and T shirts were splattered with blobs of rich purple stains, as Grandad's herd of cows breathed on me over the hedge. My favourite drink as a child was always dandelion and burdock. I seem to remember a local man delivering our order in the back of an old van. One sniff and I immediately wanted another glass. So did Granny. She was as obsessed as me with the taste. The bottles were lined up in neat rows in her kitchen. I never remember sampling that sweet, dark red liquid anywhere else, except sitting with her on a warm afternoon giggling. Now the bottles are everywhere; that magical, delicious elixir of childhood.

One of the most memorable smells of my Ulster childhood was that of the humble brown rabbit. In the countryside rabbit stew was eaten all the time. Bubbling away in a pot on an old cream Aga, it was cheap to make and very tasty. Sometimes on a dark morning, huddled up under the eiderdown on the lumpy mattress, I heard the shots in the nearby fields and imagined my grandfather in his ancient leather jacket pointing the gun at the fleeing creatures. He would weave in and out of the long grass puffing on his cigarette butt, swinging his spoils. One… two… or, if we were very lucky… three for the pot. Shortly after, I would drift back to sleep, wondering how anyone could rise at dawn and trample through the countryside in the freezing cold. Later on, I would watch with a mixture of fascination and horror, as Granny would roll her sleeves up, take a deep sigh and skin the rabbit. Her fingers moved at breakneck speed, back and forth, not missing a single one. Naturally despite much persuasion I always refused to take part in this weekly ritual.

The primary school canteen was heaving with children in home-made knitted cardigans and jumpers, tartan skirts and grey woollen trousers. Shirts with frayed collars and girls' plaits sprouting from the side of heads with matching ribbons. The hungry boys plunged into their lunch, with dirty hands and faces, hardly aware of the food in front of them. Miss Sharp and Mr O'Leary hovered at each table, glaring at the noisy brats spread-eagled over each other. They waved fingers at the guilty culprits and tried to see who could tut the loudest. No child dared risk any bad behaviour until angry eyes were temporarily diverted.

Today it was Friday and fish was on the menu, followed by pink custard and jam roly-poly. For us children, it seemed worth chewing the flat, tasteless white objects sprawled on the plate. The reward of the thick slices of sponge was not that far away.

Chatting and laughing as usual, something terrible happened. *I'd swallowed a bone!* The crowded chaos of the lunch hour was spinning above my head. My flushed cheeks lost their colour. Three children opposite jumped up, stabbing their fingers in front of my nose.

"Quick Miss," one said, "Wendy's choking! She can't breathe."

"Is she going to die?" another one shouted.

"No of course not... sit down children. *Now!*"

I was spluttering and gasping so much that one of the male teachers swooped me up in his tight comforting arms. He dashed out of the canteen, and rushed over the road. I remember gazing at my scuffed red sandals dangling in the air and my skirt flapping in the breeze. Mr Smart rushed into the old building of the nearest doctor's surgery and quickly explained what had happened. Most of the horror of the occasion is now a blur. The only memory I retain is lying on a cold reclining leather chair, where a sharp instrument was manoeuvred down my throat. Miraculously the bone was removed and I burst into tears.

The teacher decided that due to the seriousness of the event, I would be allowed to spend the afternoon in the solicitor's office where my mother worked, as this was only a few doors down. Here, under the watchful eye of old Mr McCormick, the boss, I sipped warm sweet tea and devoured a whole plate of Marie biscuits. This tall, serious man was not quite sure what to make of the little blond-haired girl, perched below the stacked dusty folders of legal documents, drawing funny pictures. It was good to be fussed over for a few hours, but I have never got over the shock of the horrible fish bone sticking in my throat. On the Monday morning I crept into class as the other children crowded round jostling and pushing. They were naturally curious about my experience but I did not want to talk about it. The sympathetic teacher shooed them away, ordering her pupils to return to their multiplication tables. I slunk into my hard-backed seat gratefully, hoping my eyes would never look at another piece of fish ever again.

There was always a mad panic in the morning during the secondary school years. My mother could not be late for work and my father left early for his job in Belfast. In the tiny green kitchen at number 27, beside a three bar electric fire on the wall, my brother and I sat balancing on red Formica stools. We nibbled on chunky slices of toast and jam and slurped our mugs of strong tea, trying hard not to dip our ties into the sweet orange liquid. Before long we experienced the onslaught of the brown hair clips! As our mother fastened her thick auburn hair up for work, the majority of the grips pinged into our hot buttered toast. Somehow they managed to burrow a path underneath the soggy strawberries and melting butter.

"Be careful you don't swallow them," she said, as we tried to preserve our young lives. We remained convinced that one day, both of us would start to rattle on our way to school.

In the first term at secondary school, I clambered onto the crowded bus with all the ingredients needed for a cookery lesson. Before long, they were sloshing around at the bottom of my new black satchel. Even though they started out in neat little piles, the contents soon wriggled out of the greaseproof paper, obliterating last night's homework.

"Why does your flour always escape?" asked the teacher, melting in front of me in the extreme heat. "And why have all your currants stuck to your exercise books *again*...?" I never knew what to say in reply, so stared at the floor, until she moved on to the next person.

Cookery was the bane of my life after Maths and PE, although years later it would become a great joy. Sometimes I misread the recipe or opened the oven too soon. Once, I never even switched the 'thing' on, which involved Miss McKeown changing face colour, whilst showing me her perfect set of sharply pointed teeth. My partner, generally a good friend in other lessons, sometimes became a bossy demon in front of a tablespoon of sugar, three ounces of butter and some red colouring. She was very organised and a dab hand in the kitchen, so we were unsuitably matched. After the end product had cooled on the wire tray, it wasn't long before the familiar words were heard in my right ear.

"Now... let's divide them up, Wendy."

My heart sank as she gave herself the bigger slice of the sponge, or counted six buns for me, whilst she took twelve. There were lots of mini squabbles where I tried to regain some authority but she won every time.

"Is this all you've got?" my dad said, peering into the shallow abyss of the oblong cake tin. "I'm not giving you any more money for ingredients, if you only come home with a few buns... *and no damn currants!*"

One of my best friends lived in a village near a potato crisp factory. Did her clothes always seem to have a slight whiff of cheese and onion crisps, or was it my imagination? Does this explain my lifelong addiction to this particular variety? Between us, we decided not to have school dinners anymore, spending the money instead at the local shop. We scuttled through the gates, past the dipping horse chestnut tree, with the occasional beret hanging from the curling branches. The illicit coins were clutched in our hands and no one ever seemed to ask any questions. So for at least a term, the two of us lived on a packet of crisps, a bar of dairy milk and a bubble gum for lunch... all for an old shilling. She went back to a home cooked dinner, but I don't think I always did.

Before I had any idea of how life would change when I moved to England, I stayed for a few months with my aunt and uncle and three young cousins in County Down. My parents were training to be publicans, so daily routine became very different. Lots of early morning travel to get to school in another town and a considerable amount of homework! In many ways, despite these difficulties, I look upon this period of my life with very fond memories. The little girls were great fun and one of the pleasures was reading a chapter from the 'Magic Stone', a story I had written when I was thirteen. The sweetest words ever, were "Wendy... can you read us another one?" Naturally I had to oblige.

At the weekend, my uncle would rush into the kitchen smelling of the early morning dew and fresh manure, for his much coveted Ulster fry. A chance to tuck in and mop the juices up with a wheaten farl. *Bliss!* Nothing evokes those perfect days at Ballymoney Cottage, more than the whiff of crispy bacon in the pan and my uncle clutching his mug of steaming tea with grubby fingers.

Once, I remember, he crept in and sank slowly into one of the chairs, eyes red and tearful. He told us reluctantly, that he had run over his trusty sheep dog by mistake. The poor creature had got in the way of the back wheels of his tractor and died. We had heard it yelping in the yard. Aunty, Uncle and I sat silently eating our breakfast. No one said a word after this announcement. This was one of the saddest moments I can recall, as for a farmer, a loyal dog really was his best friend.

No reminiscing about food would be complete, without mentioning the humble cream cracker. Every evening at ten o'clock, to the sound of Big Ben chiming on ITV, footsteps could be heard on the long passageway from the kitchen. My lovely aunt would push the door open with a beaming smile and the tasty supper was delivered on a tray. A plate of crisp, cream crackers smothered with Irish butter, thick slices of cheddar cheese and gleaming slices of fresh red tomatoes. Three cups of steaming hot chocolate to wash it down. *Magic!*

On those occasions I tried my best to be ladylike, as I dived into the contents of my plate, trying hard not to scatter the crumbs. We settled into the old couch… us three, laughing and nibbling, with the small black and white TV in the corner delivering the latest news. My three young cousins slept soundly upstairs, and soon with a full tummy I would creep up to join them, avoiding the wonky stair in the middle.

14

Leaving

June 1968. The end of term arrived and my final day. The red sun exploded over the factory wall behind the thin curtains. Adult voices drifted through the open windows as their offspring were cajoled into waking up. I glanced at the school uniform lying on the bed. Was this the last time I would ever wear it? The baggy navy gym slip, the frayed tie, (but only on the edges) and the blue cotton shirt with the button missing at the top. A navy beret. One of many. Most of these were yanked off heads and usually thrown in hedges. I peeped outside and noticed the flower beds for the last time. The rich striking colours of the dahlias and geraniums. The tiered garden ambling down to the lawn, where we had posed for photographs over the years. The bushy fir trees in a perfect line near the fence.

My brother and I sat side by side in the tiny kitchen at the back, surrounded by tea chests. We nibbled our toast and jam seeking out those rogue hair clips and slurped our mugs of tea. He attended a different school, but like me was apprehensive about starting a new life. Outside, Dad was warming up the engine and beeping the horn, near the pale pink magnolia tree. We were always running late. Mum stood, arms folded in the doorway in her delightful summer dress. She waved as we drove off.

I slid onto the cream leather seat, and thought about the occasion a few weeks ago, when my arrival at school had caused embarrassment. I was late for an important lesson. Behind us there were flashing blue lights! In the 1960s there weren't many cars on the road so being followed was more noticeable. We screeched into the car park and I was mortified! Everyone stared and pointed.

"Duck down Wendy," Dad shouted, noticing my flushed cheeks.

Without any hesitation I crumpled into a tiny ball behind his seat. A policeman sauntered up to the car and my dad wound down the window.

"Is this your car sir?" He was about to mention the speed of the vehicle, when he saw me. "Who's that?" His face registered surprise.

"My daughter!"

"What's she doing down there?"

Before I could utter a word, Dad threw open the door and I scampered off to join all the late stragglers. I was convinced our Headteacher would mention the incident in assembly... but fortunately he didn't. Phew!

Today though, it was just Dad and me, with lots of fond memories spinning round in my head. For him, future prospects were exciting and he couldn't stop talking about them. He was going to be running his own pub, something he had always wanted to do.

"A new adventure is on our horizon," he said, depositing me safely this time, inside the gate.

I felt sad all day sauntering from one lesson to the other, alongside those close friends whom I would soon be parted from. Each teacher uttered a few kind comments about my imminent departure. All I could think of was what scheme I could conjure up so I could stay. Sadly my imagination produced no answers.

That morning our devoted headteacher was scurrying down the corridor in his black gown, in the usual friendly manner. I wondered if he knew I was leaving, being one of those people who was fond of all his charges. *My last day at secondary school.* The place I loved which had introduced me to so many diverse subjects. Hard to believe this moment had arrived. That was that! *The grand finale.* When you're 15 nothing really sinks in. Events on the horizon don't seem real. A bit of a fantasy, like my favourite book Alice in Wonderland. Perhaps I really was Alice. There were many hugs and tears. Addresses scribbled on pieces of paper torn out of jotters. Promises to write shortly and tell friends what the girls were like in England. I didn't realise at the time, but the answer to that would be 'very kind, confident and a bit more sophisticated'.

At lunch time we gathered on the step for an important photograph. The bright sunshine sparkled on our faces. A couple of us knelt down and smiled at the camera. I remember thinking: 'This is it Wendy!' I peeped over the empty playing fields with the circling black crows and remembered myself lying on the pitch. At three thirty with head buzzing, lumps bouncing in my throat, the old jalopy pulled out of the school drive and all those special friends who meant so much scattered. The ones I laughed with, played hockey with, or wrote 'I love Paul McCartney' on an exercise book in class with. I realised I would miss seeing the navy beret clinging to the ends of the horse chestnut branches but I wouldn't be sorry to leave behind the whiff of carbolic in the lukewarm showers. I would always remember the fascinating History of Art lessons, learning about Shakespeare's life or enjoying fabulous French. But Maths and Science would remain a mystery to me. I would remember above all the teachers who were inspirational and those who hadn't been.

Our family travelled over to England on the Belfast to Liverpool boat. Overnight, in a squashed cabin, with all our tea-chests and possessions in the hold. It felt strange to be with parents I hadn't seen or talked to for months. They had been busy training to be publicans and in those days children had to be left behind during this process. I crept up onto the top deck to be on my own and stared out at the vanishing coastline, as the packed boat slowly left the Irish shores. I was transported back to the last games of hopscotch outside number 27. Red sandals scattering the chalk and tiny stones. I smiled at the thought of the vicar jumping over the soap suds on our tarmac drive. Billy's fondness for the cream feather boa still made me giggle. The twinkling lights of Belfast Harbour and all those childhood memories would never be forgotten, as we made our way further and further out to sea. I knew that one day they would be written down somewhere. The cold air zapped my face and the icy spray flew over the slippery deck as I clung on to the rail. I didn't want to go down to our cabin until the land had disappeared completely.

A new life lay ahead over the Irish Sea. Goodbye Ulster...

About the Author

Wendy Breckon grew up in Ulster and left Irish shores at the age of fifteen and a half. The memory of the fading lights twinkling in Belfast Harbour still makes her feel nostalgic. She spent her childhood somersaulting and tumbling in the farmyards and fields of County Down, pursued by many lively cousins, giggling and seeking adventure.

After the sixth form a secret dream came true! For one year she worked in Fleet Street on Printing Trades Journal. During this creative period she became a prolific poet.

Wendy fondly remembers a brief stint in John Lewis, in Oxford Street, before her teaching career began, where out of boredom, she once chased a Russian shop-lifter down many escalators before losing her completely. When the children were small, Wendy was thrilled to be a part-time journalist for the Hertfordshire Mercury. The recollection of trundling through country lanes with a clipboard, in her red 2CV, still makes her smile.

For a few years, she organised drama workshops, in infant and junior schools, on mime, improvisation and storytelling. Her favourite moment will always be the one where she dressed up as a giant in the Irish legend of Finn MacCool. Eventually, Wendy took up the position of Head of Drama in a Hertfordshire secondary school, a career she loved passionately.

Her affection for the performing arts first materialised in the fifth form, where the part of Hermia in Midsummer Night's Dream gave her the taste for greasepaint and sparkle. She also auditioned with a friend in the sixth form, for the National Youth Theatre in front of Sir Michael Croft.

A decade ago, Wendy arrived in the West Country with her husband

Peter. Living eight minutes from Lyme Regis and the sea, the creative juices exploded. Apart from writing her memoir, she has been successful in local performance events. These have included winning the Bridport Story Slam twice and the Poole Story Slam once. Taking part in the 'Apothecary' and 'Vittles & Verse' alongside others is always great fun.

One of the stories in this book, 'The Russian Princess', came 3rd in the 2016 Winchester memoir competition. Two short stories of a different genre were chosen to be included in 'This Little World', an anthology published by the Dorset Writers Network. She was also commended in 'The Words for the Wounded' short story competition, organised by the on-line Frost Magazine, to which Wendy has previously contributed many lively articles.

Wendy looks forward to her regular trips to Ireland and London, to see the family. Perfect inspiration can be found in Skerries her second favourite place by the sea.

About the Publisher

Magic Oxygen Limited is a little green publishing house based in Lyme Regis, Dorset. It was founded in 2011 by Tracey and Simon West, who share an enormous passion for organic seasonal food, simple green living and advocating sustainable behaviours in local and global environments; they also share a common love of the written word. They've published titles from some remarkable authors, including Bridport Prize winning Chris Hill and the much loved children's writer, Sue Hampton.

See MagicOxygen.co.uk/shop and remember, all of their titles can be ordered from your favourite High Street bookshops and online too. They urge you to visit nearby independent retailers to place your orders. When you spend money with them, you'll help keep it in your local community.

About the Word Forest Organisation

The Word Forest Organisation is an NGO started by Magic Oxygen founders, Tracey and Simon West. Its primary function is planting trees and raising environmental awareness in the Coast Province of Kenya which is helping to improve the health of our planet and all its inhabitants.

Trees planted in this tropical region are incredibly efficient at drawing down and locking in CO_2 and other pollutants and keeping the planet a little cooler. Their forests are also helping to reduce the devastating effects of climate change, encouraging the normal rains to fall and relieving the problems from Kenya's ongoing drought.

Visit WordForest.org to become a member, donate, or buy the ideal gift of trees for a loved one to celebrate a birthday, anniversary, or perhaps even to commemorate a life.

#legacygift

Coming in Wendy's second book...

Chapter 1

A Bit of a Shock

Sunny skies. A tiny car park. Animated people laughing and chatting, sprawled underneath red stripy umbrellas in a pub garden. One day, in early September 1968. The removal van pulled up abruptly, spitting out its occupants on the sticky tarmac. My brother almost fell into a tea chest marked Valuables. My mother skidded on a pile of Enid Blyton books. I narrowly avoided landing on some serious drinkers enjoying the spectacle.

"Well, here it is love. Your dream. Roses round the door," my mother announced.

"Yes... perfect," my father muttered, wondering if the advertisement in the Daily Express, might have contained a slight exaggeration.

The lounge bar seemed cosy and intimate. Dusty plastic flowers perched in a vase on the window sill and one or two faded hunting scenes hung on the wall. People balanced on the ends of their stools, puffing curls of nicotine and peering into glasses of lager or Dubonnet with lemonade. The whiff of stale beer and smoke made my nostrils twitch. The music emanating from the square box in the corner was a compilation including Englebert Humperdink, Tom Jones, The Beatles, and Mary Hopkin. I remember Mary because her sweet gentle voice singing 'Those were the days my friend. We thought they'd never end,' greeted me, as I scanned the room trying to imagine living in a pub. Such a contrast from being surrounded by an eccentric Granny in a Cossack hat, squawking chickens, the sound of tractors and dripping milk churns. Looking back, I now realise that I went into shock for the first six months.

"We're very fortunate with the music." The barman told us smugly. "You don't have to think about changing anything. There are twenty tunes and they play all day back to back."

I tried to work out how many times each day, I would have to listen to Mary Hopkin and Tom Jones.

My bedroom was above the public bar. It was quite cramped with damp green wallpaper. I didn't mind having a bed squashed up in the corner and a threadbare mat, when I saw the floor to ceiling book shelves. Pure Joy! The Famous Five and Secret Seven collectibles would soon be restored to glory. My younger brother, when looking for mischief, used to pull all the books onto the floor; but that's another story.

At about 11.00pm every evening I managed to drift off to sleep... exhausted. Little did I know, apart from the delightful Mary Hopkin lyrics floating through the floor boards, that the sound of pinging darts on the board would keep me awake every night. This was before I'd even experienced the expletives, the raised voices and the occasional drunken exchange. Cotton wool in ears became a nightly event.

Opposite our pub was the secondary school I attended and a smaller building off to the left, the local youth club. On my very first tentative visit to the Monday evening session, one of the girls rushed up to me, in a very friendly manner.

"I love this record, don't you Wendy?" she shouted, as I joined the circle of girls, long hair, like mine, parted in the middle.

I wore a 60's black ribbed jumper and an orange mini skirt from Etam. The song was sweet and gentle and a catchy little number.

"Oh yes, I know that one," I replied, pulling a face, as we danced around our handbags in the middle of the floor. As Mary sang her heart out, I remember wondering if she was going to follow me around for the rest of my teenage life.

Lightning Source UK Ltd.
Milton Keynes UK
UKOW01f1245180717
305537UK00002B/87/P